BRING YOUR A-GAME......
EVEN IF YOU'RE JUST STARTING OUT!

AN ENTREPRENEUR'S GUIDE TO GROWNING AND MANAGING SOCIAL MEDIA PLATFORMS.

Copyright

ISBN: **9781983049668**

TABLE OF CONTENTS

INTRODUCTION

Do you sometimes look at the big brands on Instagram and Facebook and feel jealous? Do you wish that you could earn a living doing the things you love and posting about it? Would you love the fame that can come from having a personal brand? Would you love to be able to earn money from a business that you created, instead of having to go into work every day? What exactly does it take to get there? And can anyone do it?

The answer is that anyone truly can build a massive online brand and gain hundreds of thousands of followers. But while this is true, it's also true that it isn't easy. It's going to take work and determination and it's going to take a good plan... The first thing to recognize is that you need to choose the right niche. You need to choose an industry that you absolutely love and that you are happy to work at every single day. If you don't truly love the niche you pick, then you will grow uninterested and you'll stop earning from it as a result. Choosing the right niche is important because if you want to have a highly successful brand and make a living from it, then you need to treat it as though it is already your living. In other words, you need to put in full-time work and you need to post consistently with high quality content on all your channels.

Once you've created your brand and chosen a niche, you're passionate about, you should make sure that all of your business accounts are public and start building on those strong foundations with regular posts. The good news is that this part is not complicated. In fact, you can follow my simple daily blueprint in order to be highly successful:

Every Weekday:

- Post at least one Instagram picture, ideally two or three. Keep a folder on your computer filled with lots of old content, so that you have something to publish on days when you don't have anything exciting to share.

- At least once every two days add some form of direct communication - such as an image on Instagram stories or a Facebook Live video.

- Integrate your accounts so that your pictures also appear on Twitter and Facebook. This will save you a ton of time from posting you content on all your social channels.

- Post at least one tweet to Twitter per day, ideally 2-3 times. Likewise, have a selection of tweets you can share on days when inspiration does not strike.

- Twice a week, write two blog posts (minimum 500 words) and post it to your blog. Promote that through your other social media accounts (Facebook and Twitter).

- Post at least one video on YouTube per week. Promote this on your other social media channels.

- Once a week, write one 'guest post' and try to get it published on other big blogs.

- Spend at least 10 minutes each morning liking other people's posts on Instagram, Facebook or Twitter.

- Spend 10 minutes promoting old blog posts on forums, social sharing sites etc.

- Send one email per week updating your audience on what you are working on.

You can do all this by only spending about 1.5 to 2 hours a day. If you can find the time, then you will find that you can very quickly grow a big audience. It really is that simple, it just takes commitment.

4 Things To Think About Before Doing A Joint Venture

Joint ventures in business are a wonderful thing. They can allow you to make money you wouldn't otherwise be able to make on your own, they enable you to tap into other people's expertise and knowledge, and potentially they can speed up projects, whilst making them more successful and sharing some of the risk. Joint ventures are talked about a great deal in the internet marketing world, but despite the many benefits there are also a number of drawbacks. Here are 5 things to think about before doing a joint venture:

1. Joint ventures mean shared profit

Say you decide to join forces with another marketer and create your own product together. You can share some of the development costs and utilize both of your respective expertise, however assuming the joint venture is split straight down the middle then it also means you'll only make half of what you would if it was solely your own product. Of course, in many scenarios this is irrelevant because the project might have been impossible on your own, but it's something to think about.

2. Joint ventures can go wrong

It can be the case that your joint venture partner simply doesn't share the same commitment to the project as you do. This can be extremely frustrating if you're putting in lots of hard work yourself and your partner simply doesn't do their bit.

3. Before you start, make sure you have an agreed timetable

It is all too easy for a joint venture project to slip behind schedule because your partner is not good at doing things on time (relating back to the point above) or simply that you both have other commitments and the project never gets finished. Before you start make sure you agree a timetable that both of you are happy with and are sure you can commit to.

4. Choose your joint venture partners carefully

Are you compatible with the other party? Should you even be considering working together? There is little point in doing a joint venture with someone who has a completely different skill set or way of thinking. Whilst joint ventures allow you to tap into other people's expertise, it is also essential that you have SOME shared knowledge, skills or common ground since otherwise the venture will become impossible. Similarly, it is usually of little value to join forces with someone who has exactly the same skill set or market access as yourself. If, for example, you have a product but no list to sell it to then look to joint venture with someone who has a list but no product to sell to them!

Getting Started as a Freelance Writer

Many people find the idea of becoming a freelancer very appealing. You can work from home and take on as much or as little work as you like. Getting started as a freelance writer however can be difficult. If you are new to the scene it is hard to win business because nobody knows who you are or what your writing ability is like.

Here are a few ways to do it (there are others but this one seems to work well!)

1. Write a sample article to show to prospective clients. Make sure it is the best you can do. Spend time perfecting it and making sure that it is grammatically correct.

2. Go over to the Warrior forum and post a WSO (a Warrior Special Offer) advertising your service. Offer a really attractive rate to get people to try you out and include your sample article within the advert so that people can see that you write to a decent standard. I would suggest a price of around $1 for every 100 words as a starting point. That should get you some initial clients.

3. Once you have completed some orders get testimonials from your clients. If they are happy with the work, you produce they should be more than willing to do this.

4. Relist your WSO, this time including the testimonials.

5. After a few weeks send a follow-up email to your previous clients asking if they have any more work for you. A lot of the people you write for will always be in need of content and will have plenty of work for you.

6. Set yourself up with a website. Give plenty of samples and include some details about yourself and your initial experience.

7. Rinse and repeat. Each time you do this you will be gaining new clients and building a relationship with your existing ones. Over time you should find that your reputation builds (assuming of course that you produce good quality work) and as it does you can begin to charge more money.

There are of course other ways of getting started as a freelance writer. Sites such as Elance can also offer a fruitful way of getting freelance work, but I hope that this article has given you some food for thought. Being a freelance writer can be hard work, but it can also be extremely rewarding. For many people it provides an easy way of making money online, even if it is just as a way of funding your other business activities.

How To Create an Interview Product

Production creation is something which many people struggle with when starting an online business. Getting the information to actually put into a product can be difficult, as can be finding the time to write or produce it. A great way of creating a quality product quickly however is to do an interview with an expert in your niche and then package it up as a product...

The benefits of doing this are massive. Providing you find the right person to interview you should be getting access to an instant pool of knowledge which can go into your product.

The first step is to find your interviewee. This is not as difficult as it sounds either because they get tons of free exposure and the chance to sell themselves, meaning that many people will jump at the chance to be interviewed! Approach people in your niche and ask them. You can find them in the usual places like blogs, forums, etc. The next thing to decide is what format you want to conduct the interview in:

You could firstly do an email interview. You simply email over your questions and let the other person respond in paragraphs, and then put the interview responses into a report or eBook. This is something I've done quite successfully in the past.

The other option is to do a 'live' interview and then record it. This could be done over Skype or telephone for example. Of course, this has the advantage in that you can create two products out of the interview - the audio recording, and the transcript of the audio recording. If you choose this option, it's always best to pre-plan and have a guide in front of you so as you know what you're going to talk about in the interview. You also need to let the other person know what you want to talk about in advance so that they can do a bit of pre-planning for the interview too.

Thinking of questions or topics to discuss:

This is easy - just think about what people in your niche want to know. If you don't know what's hot then just take a look at forums, blogs, or websites in your niche. For example, people in the internet marketing niche might want to know how he/she would build a list, or how they got started with an online business. Ask questions about the hot topics in your niche and you won't go far wrong with your interview.

However, you decide to do it, creating an interview product is one of the easiest ways of creating a product, and it's also one of the best because you should end up with a product that is genuinely of high quality.

Using WSOs To Build Your List

We all know that 'the money is in the list' but actually building your list can be a struggle, especially if you are new to internet marketing. So how would you like to start building your list TODAY? I'm being serious here. Follow the article below and you'll be on your way to creating what is probably the single most valuable asset an internet marketer can have. The method I'm about to detail involves creating a WSO (a Warrior Special Offer) ...

What is a WSO?

The Warrior Special Offer Forum is a special section of the Warrior forum, an online community for internet marketers, where you can post what are effectively paid ads. The only thing to bear in mind is that your offer must be better or cheaper than that is available to the general public.

Using WSOs to build your list.

Step 1: Create a product of value. You're going to give this away to people who join your list. It doesn't have to be anything fancy, but make sure it is something other internet marketers will want and that it has a catchy title.

Step 2: Create your squeeze page. This is where people will subscribe to your list, and ideally it should have graphics. Sell your product to people as though they are going to be paying for it.

Step 3: Create an upsell. It costs money to post a WSO ($20) but it's well worth it, and if you stick an upsell behind your offer, you'll make money AND build your list.

Step 3: Post your WSO. Link to your squeeze page and make sure people know it is a freebie. Again, sell your offer as though it is paid...

That's it! Using WSOs to build your list is one of the most effective things you can do online. Get it right and you should see opt-ins coming in within minutes of posting your offer.

Why is it so effective?

Quite simply the Warrior forum gets THOUSANDS of visitors every day and they are all highly targeted ones too. Using WSOs to build your list can kick start your efforts in an instant. Try it and you'll be hooked.

How To Produce a Good Squeeze Page

Many would argue that the ability to produce a good squeeze page is a bit of an art form. This is true – but as long as you keep some basic principles in mind it shouldn't be too difficult for even a newbie to create a squeeze page that converts at a decent rate.

First of all, what IS a squeeze page?

Quite simply it's a single webpage where people enter their name and email address in order to join your list. This is usually in return for some sort of freebie – whether it's a report, eBook package, or a set of videos. The sole purpose of a squeeze page is to get people to opt-in to your list. That's it. It shouldn't have any other function that might 'distract' the reader.

Tip # 1 – Give away a quality freebie

There was a time when you could offer a free report on pretty much anything and people would sign up for it simply because it was free. This isn't the case anymore. People are becoming more and more choosey about what they will swap their name and email address for, so the first step towards producing a good squeeze page is to make sure your freebie is of good quality and is something people in your niche will actually want.

Tip # 2 – Make sure your copy makes your freebie 'irresistible'

If your offering is something people will want, AND they know they want it - they will sign up. Your copy should pull out all the juicy bits of what they will receive and make it such that they simply can't turn down your freebie.

Tip # 3 – Have a catchy title

We have all seen free reports been given away with the title "10 top tips to......." In the current internet world this is seen as BORING. Give your product a catchy title and make it stand out. Take a look at the bestselling products in your niche and look at the sorts of product names they use.

Tip # 3 – Use graphics to "sell" your product

Make your squeeze page look like a paid product. Spend the time or invest money into creating good quality graphics. In my opinion this is the most important step towards producing a good squeeze page. Of course, there are plenty of them out there which have no graphics at all (and it seems to be an increasingly popular trend) but if you take that route then you need to be able to write really good copy. If you use graphics, your copy won't need to be as good and it'll still convert at a decent rate.

The Power of Testimonials

Convincing people that your product or service is actually any good can be difficult, especially online where people may have been burned in the past. Most people won't buy from you without some sort of pre-existing relationship, and anything that boosts your credibility can clearly only be a good thing. Before people invest in your product or opt-in to your list, they want to be sure that they aren't wasting their time or money. This is why testimonials are so powerful - they have far more credibility than anything you write yourself simply because they are someone else's opinion.

So how do you get testimonials? Start by getting into the habit of asking anyone who buys from you to give you their opinion. If your product or service is actually of good quality, then the feedback you get should be overwhelmingly positive. Try producing a short questionnaire and send it to all your customers. Obviously not everyone will oblige, but those who do may give you valuable quotes that you can use as testimonials in your business.

Another strategy is to give away copies of your product to other marketers on the basis that they will give you their honest opinion – and make sure it is honest as well! It is quite easy to get people to give you testimonials since it is free advertising for the other person and boosts their own credibility.

Where should you include testimonials? You should definitely put them onto your sales pages and squeeze pages, but there are other places too – in emails to your list or posts on your blog.

You can also go beyond the testimonial by producing case studies. Has one of your customers had a success story because of your product? If you can produce a good case study, you'll help people to understand more about your offering, whilst also re-assuring them that it is the right thing for them. Case studies can make excellent press releases too, giving your online PR a boost and getting you some valuable free advertising and coverage in the media if your press release gets picked up by publications.

What Can Coaching Do For You and Your Business?

Starting an online business is a huge learning curve. The idea is initially very exciting, but soon the excitement and interest can turn into frustration and confusion as you plough your way through a minefield of information. It's all too easy to suffer massive information overload and give up the online dream before you have even started.

Does the following sound familiar? You buy an information product, read it, and think to yourself 'I'll put this into action.' The next day another offer plops into your inbox, you buy it, read it, and again you start to feel excited that 'this is the one.' A few days later and you've completely forgotten about that product, you buy into the next big launch... and so the cycle continues.

Why is this? It's partly the dream and idea that there is a magic button or silver bullet out there; a big 'secret' that if you find it, you'll become rich. The other reason is information overload and not knowing where to begin.

How do you get out of this cycle? For many people the answer is mentoring. By finding a good coach you literally have someone to hold you by the hand, 'join the dots' for you, and ensure that you stay focused. By working closely with someone who is themselves already successful you stand a much greater chance of achieving success yourself. Reading an information product or strategy and actually doing it are two completely different things. Often things sound easy but implementing them is a whole different story. If you have a mentor there to guide and support, you they can ensure you get up and running quickly.

Some people argue that success breeds success and I can't help but agree. If you're struggling online, then getting a good coach may be one of the best decisions you ever make.

Writing a Good Autoresponder Sequence

So, you've got people to opt-in to your list and you're building a subscriber base. This is probably the single most important thing you can do in your online business BUT if you don't follow it up with a good autoresponder sequence then you're pretty much putting all of your list building efforts to waste…

A good autoresponder sequence builds a relationship with your subscribers. It (hopefully) gets them to buy products from you and engage in what you're all about. Many people get it wrong. They stack up the messages without giving much thought to what they are actually doing. Here's how to do it right:

1. Put yourself in your subscribers' shoes

Easier said than done I agree, but do you really want to be receiving sales email after sales email each and every day? The first step towards writing a good autoresponder sequence is to put yourself in your subscribers' shoes and think about what they would like to receive. What interests them? What will benefit them?

2. Give content. Don't just sell.

It's a funny thing but the truth is that the less you sell, the more you'll sell! Give quality content in your autoresponder sequence and look out for your subscribers' interests. Tell stories, give them helpful advice that they can put into action straight away without needing to buy anything.

3. Carefully time your emails

Autoresponders let you space your messages in any way you wish. All you have to do for each message is to specify the number of days between that email and the last one. Try delivering them every day for the first few days, and then space them out a little longer after say the first week. Why? Because immediately after subscribing people are 'hot' about you and it's a great time to sell to them.

4. Think about what they originally signed up for

Most people build their list by giving away some sort of freebie in return for the opt-in. A top tip for writing a good autoresponder sequence is to make sure that your emails relate back to the original thing they signed up to receive. If your squeeze page 'bait' was about blogging, then they are obviously interested in blogging or they wouldn't have subscribed!

Above all – give quality content and deliver to your subscriber's content that you know they will enjoy. Take a look at other marketer's autoresponder sequences. How do THEY do it?

Why Build a Membership Site?

Membership sites seem to be all the rage in internet marketing circles. Let's face it – you can barely open your inbox without seeing an offer promoting the launch of yet ANOTHER new membership site or continuity program. So, what's all the fuss about? Why build a membership site?

Let me start by saying that if you are an internet marketer and you DON'T yet have your own membership site, you are missing out... big time.

The main benefit is that it gives you a recurring income (and I am sure you'll agree this is a massive plus point! You get paid each and every month for as long as the person remains a member of your site. One subscriber paying you $27 a month is worth $324 to you over the course of a single year, and here is the best bit – you only have to sell to them ONCE. How much easier is that than trying to sell to the same people over and over again? All you need to do is to get them to continue their membership by providing quality content. This is much, much easier than selling.

You will of course find that people cancel their memberships. It doesn't matter how fantastically amazing your website is – it WILL happen and in fairly large numbers too. But whilst we're on that topic just take a moment to think about this - if you recruit more people each month than you lose then your income is going to rise each month. This is very cool stuff and once you have a continuity program, you'll be addicted to them and the possibilities they bring for your business.

There are other benefits too. Build a membership site and you'll also build a very strong relationship with your members. It helps you to be seen as an authority source in your niche and builds your credibility, and they are also very attractive to affiliates. They too are compelled to promote your product for the chance to earn a recurring income.

If I was starting out from scratch today as an internet marketer one of the first things, I would do is build a membership site. It gives you the security of a regular income and there are absolutely vast amounts of money to be made if you are offering the right sort of content for your target market.

SNAPCHAT

More and more entrepreneurs are starting to use Snapchat to market their products, gain more clients and up their visibility. It is one of the hottest social media platforms for millennials right now that supports more than 20 languages, so if your target market happens to be 40 and under then you need to be utilizing this free app. Contrary to popular belief Snapchat is a powerhouse marketing tool with tons of content being shared every second. Most businesses that market on social media use Facebook and Instagram but only 2% are actively engaging on Snapchat. With the lack of competition your business has a great opportunity to flourish and stand out, bringing you more potential income. The key is to know who your target market is, when you know what they want and what they like, connecting with them is easier. With Snaps you only have a few seconds to make a lasting impression, so you will need to get your point across by producing some memorable, brand building content that stands out.

Unlike the many other social platforms, it doesn't matter when you post your content on Snapchat, your snaps will not get overlooked on a busy timeline. Your snaps stay unopened until your followers view them. After your viewers open your snaps, they are only available for 24 hours after being posted.

The key to snapchat is consistency, so start by planning what you will use your account for, what you will show and how you will keep your followers engaged. Such as creating tutorials about something in your area of expertise, giving a behind the scenes at your store or workspace, and showing the quality of your product. Sharing a behind the scenes show the process that you use for business and helps your followers become invested in your brand. It shows them your passion and the hard work that you put into your brand. Pay close attention to the content that you are sharing and make sure that your brand is not faceless. Give your snaps some personality by sharing some personal tidbits of yourself and your family, the holidays are a great time to incorporate this by showing how you and your family prepare, decorate and spend your holidays.

In the past 24 hours, I have learned what the weather is like in Paris, got details about a free webinar, found a new online boutique, and watched a sunset in Canada. Today I shared a snap of my Pug, my first cup of coffee, a video of me and my son dancing, back 2 school shopping, website updates and an inspirational quote. It is imperative that you be yourself and incorporate your brands core values into your snaps.

*Over 400 Million Snaps are being shared daily

*Research shows that Snapchat now has more users than Twitter

*80% of Snapchat users are millennials

*70% of smartphone users are Snapchatters

If you are anything like me, when I first made an account, I was so lost. I had no clue how to use the geofilter feature, how to share my pictures or 10 second video to My Story, which is basically your timeline. Stories are multiple images or videos that surround a topic. It took some getting use to but after leaving my followers hanging for weeks at a time, I decided to give it a real chance and was shocked at the number of messages I started receiving pertaining to my products.

For bloggers and brands, it is essential to allow anyone to view your snaps because you cannot grow if you are not seen. Make sure your settings are set so that your story is public, allowing everyone to see what you chose to share. When you first signup you are automatically set to private, so make sure to change your settings.

Be mindful of creating snaps that keep people coming back for more. Content that is creative but logical, interesting to your followers and makes sense from your brands standpoint. If you are a fashion blogger it probably wouldn't do you any good to send out snaps of food every day. If you do snap food, make sure its relevant to your viewers by snapping other pics to your story. Perhaps your visiting a new restaurant, let them know that by creating a whole story not just one single pic of your plate. You must be "OnFleek" with your snap game to get views.

Please note that there is no search option or hashtags on Snapchat to find users, you must manually add people by their username or phone number. Therefore, your followers wanted to follow you and knew one of those two things to add you. The easiest way for you to add followers is by adding them from your address book. Go to the apps home screen, tap Add Friends and then click on Contacts. From there you can add the contacts that are stored in your phone. Once you add someone, they will receive a notification prompting them to add you back. The app also offers a chat option for you to communicate with snappers via text. If you have a blog or business, make sure you are being creative with sharing your snap profile on your other social media platforms, newsletters and blogs to gain a wide arrange of followers. This is important because you may be snapping some great content but if it is not getting in front of people then you're wasting precious marketing material.

You can create a fun graphic that shares your username, using your colors, fonts and other elements of your brand. Include a caption that states what type of things you snap that may interest people. You can also share your direct URL, it makes it so much easier for people who want to follow you.

The goal is to have a good time so use the app to show the fun side of your business. Play around with filters and come up with some catchy captions. Snapchat is the perfect platform to show the human side of your business. Share your expertise surrounding your business and have your audience reply to your snaps. Make sure you are responding as well; its social media so be social. I found a good way to engage with my viewers was to ask them to share pictures and videos of them wearing my brand and in return I would send out snaps featuring them. It makes your customers feel valued and it also helps potential buyers feel more comfortable with purchasing from you. I have saw Sephora use this method with sweepstakes. They asked their viewers to take pictures of themselves with makeup doodles and post them on their other social media platforms.

Do not be afraid to repurpose content from your other social media sites, just make sure it fits the fun and casual tone that snapchat has and remember that no social feed should be 100% promotion. Share some interesting stories related to your niche, show people your family outings, your work area, what book you are currently reading and so forth to make people feel as though they have a personal connection to you. Make sure you are following people back and replying when appropriate, this lets your viewers know that you're a real person behind a brand.

GET CREATIVE

You can create custom geofilters for your business using photoshop or Canva. It should have a width of 1080 pixels and a height of 1920 pixels. Make sure that the background is transparent and save it as a PNG. Another unique experience that businesses are creating for their viewers is creating a sponsored snapchat lens. This will give your product a fun twist and your users will be advertising your brand for free every time they use your filter and post their pictures to their other social media accounts.

Use text, emojis and draw or write on your pictures to add humor. Dove has used this strategy to inspire their fans to celebrate their own beauty. In the snap the company drew on images with bold colors to bring emphasize to their message. I have also saw company's collect reply snaps and share them back through their story.

Find unique ways to get people to pay attention. Take GrubHub for instance. They used a series of images showing a pizza being eaten slice by slice to hold our attention while creating suspense that lead up to them revealing a discount code in the last image. Very clever.

Tell a short story using a series of snaps. If you are using photos rather than videos, add music as an incentive. It may be wise to state that you do not own the rights to the music. I know this has become a big deal on Facebook and they will delete your post or suspend your account, just to be on the safe side save yourself the trouble and make the statement. You may also want to think about captivating your audience by creating how to videos or DIY skits that they can follow and interact with.

Create a call to action by asking your viewers to take a screenshot of your snap. Example: Send a snap stating that you are about to give out an exclusive discount code and that they should take a screenshot of it. Then send out another snap of you revealing the code. You can also ask your followers to visit your website but make sure to give them so sort of incentive for doing so. Example: Start a story on your snap and then tell them that it is continued on your blog and snap your web address. Try creating a snap with a call to action like "15% off today only". These enticements encourage your audience to shop while making them feel as though they are in the loop of exclusive offers that other customers do not have access too.

Deliver private content to your audience that they wouldn't see on your other social media platforms. Such as sneak peaks on new inventory or you working behind the scenes at a fashion show. Giving limited time offers will have your viewers running to your website to catch the sale before it ends (add your link to your snap) or reward them at the end of a snap story for them being loyal. Administering a contest will have them coming back to check your snap daily and possibly telling a friend about the giveaway or whatever incentive you are offering.

Customize your content by adding filters and stickers that are on available for your geographic location, a live event you are attending, and the holiday themes are huge. The spontaneous factor is why Snapchat is becoming additive to so many at such a fast pace, it creates a realistic viewpoint and it's just plain ole fun. With snaps you can document your entire day to keep your followers engaged without being annoying.

You could create weekly snap-segments on a particular day that gives your viewers something to look forward to, launch a new product and give them the chance to view it before anyone else and send your new followers a personal snap to say thank you. To gain more followers on Snapchat you could send out an alert on your other social sites that you are revealing a new product or unboxing an item that you will be giving away only on Snapchat, make sure to leave your link or QR code.

Encourage your supporters to continue viewing your snaps by alerting them that you will be posting coupon codes and hidden info in your content. You could have them screenshot a certain snap and bring it to your store location or tweet the photo for a $5 off discount. To present a coupon, you can take a picture of a physical coupon or flyer that you have had made or you can create a specific coupon just for Snapchat with a unique discount code such as 15% off your online order, use code: snap18. Hide secret code words in your snaps and have followers enter the word at checkout for exclusive deals. I did this once as a promotion for my boutique. I created three discount code words and depending on which word they entered they received a different discount.

Example: Fashion = 10% off

Flawless = 20% off

Summer = 25% off

Opening up a line of communication is imperative and gives you a more personal feel to your audience. Ask your followers for their opinions, have them answer questions or take a brief survey. They can send a video or photo to respond back or via the chat feature.

Consider creating a video of someone modeling your brand or demoing your merchandise to show how it works or to generate buzz around a product that you will be releasing soon. Hair stylist can ask their followers to send in photos of their current favorite hair trends for a chance to win a service or gift certificate. This strategy brings suspense and excitement to your watchers and makes them feel emotionally connected to you and your brand, which will lead to repeat customers, positive reviews and word of mouth advertising to their family and friends.

Online marketing has become the best way to get the word out about upcoming products, services or events. Producing a snap story allows you to broadcast your event and gives an insider view for those people who may not live close enough to attend the event. Use your snap story to post videos of you explaining why people should attend your event, the benefits, time, date and location. You can also use this opportunity to direct your viewers to your other social media pages for more information or links to register for the event. This creates involvement and excitement for your audience.

Customers love to see brand personality and what better way to do that than with videos and images tailored exclusively for Snapchat. Encourage your audience to signup for your email list (you do have an email list, right?) by mentioning a free email course, download, newsletter, exclusive deals or something that will pique their interest. You could even take a picture of your newsletter and share it as a snap to show your viewers what they can expect. Exporting your Snapchat story is also a great way to build your audience and repurpose your content on other platforms or in an email. You can save your story as a video by clicking the download icon next to your "My Story" button.

If you have a brick -and-mortar storefront, you can use a website like Sticker Mule to create decals of your snapcode and place them in areas of your store that are highly visible to your customers such as your front door next to your "We accept Visa, Mastercard, and Discover" decals. This alerts your customer that your business is on Snapchat and will likely lead to a huge boost of followers who will create content from your business and share it to their media accounts which are filled with their local friends, co-workers, neighbors and family. Placing your snapcode on your business card is an extra bonus and sends an indication to anyone that you give your card to that you are on Snapchat and want to link with them.

Incorporate a way for people to reach you in person, like creative ways of showing your business card and business phone number. Share your business and life routines, what inspires you (quotes, people, books, etc.) things you love (flowers, pets, your wardrobe, cars, etc.).

BLOGGERS

Snapchat has become a great marketing resource whether you're a blogger or not. You can connect with co-workers, friends, family, celebrities and other bloggers to get a glimpse of their real life. A great way for you to interact with your audience is by showing moments of your day to day life. Behind the scenes of a new project that you are working on, gathering data for a blog post, or you can have someone take a quick video of you publishing your blog post. After publishing you can upload a snap announcing your new article to get instant traffic to your blog. Sharing your pinable images to snapchat also grabs your viewers attention and creates a call to action for them to head over to your blogsite to read the article.

Show your real personality, your hobbies, weird habits, your quirks and things that you are passionate about such as bird watching if that's your thing. Hosting a blogger Q&A is also a unique way to get your followers engaged. You may not be able to answer all the questions that you receive, however your viewers should leave feeling as though they received some valuable information after watching your Q&A story. You may opt to send personal chats to answer their questions or you can simply comment on their photo or video with your reply. This strategy is great to connect with other bloggers and brands to make yourself visible and possibly start a networking relationship.

Add your Snapcode on your blogsite or the Snapchat logo and link it directly to your profile to make it super easy for your readers to connect with you on Snapchat. Create a call to action by placing a Connect with Us or Follow Us widget on the sidebar of your blog to direct traffic to your other social media platforms. Another way to increase your growth is to create an Auto-Dm campaign on Twitter. Setup your twitter account to automatically send your new twitter followers a direct message. In the message include your Snapchat URL and a call to action to follow you in Snapchat.

You may consider asking some of your customers to take over your account for a discount or for fun, this is equal to asking your customers if you can take a picture of them with your merchandise but instead ask them to take a snap. Featuring others gives people a reason to stay tuned to your snap and tell their friends and family to tune in if they know they will be in your snap story. You can also feature other businesses and locations to get some extra traffic, especially if they are a small business owner. They may give you a shout out for featuring their business which in turn will send you more followers.

To develop some ideas for a sequenced snap story I suggest that you grab a piece of paper, draw four squares and write "10 seconds" under each one. In the first square write the beginning of your story, two squares will be the middle of your story and the last square is your ending. Be funny, creative and informative. This strategy will help you to create a focused story that your viewers can follow.

Increasing your following on Snapchat does not have to be hard, especially once you know the tricks of the trade. However, growing your followers is only the beginning. You will need to continue to engage your audience with relevant content to convert them to customers once they opt in to follow you and remember authenticity is essential. It can take some getting used to but with consistency you can boost your blogs fanbase. Have fun Snapping.

YOUTUBE

In this chapter we are going to discuss the exact formulas you will need to create and crush your YouTube channel. YouTube was launched February 14, 2005 and as of 2018 it is the third most used website in the world with more than 900 million visitors a month. Savvy business started realizing that by using YouTube they could get free, targeted and organic traffic to their websites and build their email list fairly quick. It is defiantly a customer magnet. There are several reasons why you should be using YouTube for your business.

- To gain subscribers for your mailing list
- To find potential customers
- To direct traffic to your website
- To sell your products or services
- To market yourself
- To get free traffic from Google
- Monetize your channel with YouTubes partnership program

One young guitar player uploaded 12 free guitar lessons onto YouTube and started receiving a steady stream of free traffic which resulted in him building his email list to 140,000 subscribers. Once his list was established, he started marketing his video lessons for $14.99 each and began making up to $20,000 a month in income.

Uploading videos to YouTube has proved to be a legitimate way to connect to your audience, communicate ideas, share tips, video clips of seminars you attend, and short videos of you talking straight into the camera about your area of expertise. With online videos you can communicate to your customers in a way that written material can not and can lead to more people wanting to do business with you.

Once you create your account you want to make sure that name reflects your niche, brand or business. If you are going to be discussing a variety of different topics, then I suggest that you use your own name for your channel. By using your name, you have the flexibility to change your content as you wish and if people google your name your channel will be one of the top results. Next, upload a professional looking header photo and profile icon. Add the description of your channel and links to your other social media profiles, this step is important mainly because your viewer may not be an active YouTube user but is on the Facebook app daily, so make sure to drop those links. For every video that you upload to YouTube it is wise to Always include a title, description and tags. Tags are very powerful on YouTube as with Instagram, therefore when using tags try to include as many as you can to target your audience. Adding your website link to your description will also up your chances of your viewers becoming customers. Doing those three things will help people to find your video by the keywords that you used. Once you have gotten the hang of things and uploaded several videos you will want to group your videos in categories and create a playlist grouping all your relevant videos to one category. Using this technique will increase the chance of a viewer watching more than one of your videos.

A lot of Vloggers like to start their videos with an introduction of who they are, what they do and why their viewers should be following them. This strategy could kill the whole vibe of your video and your viewer may leave before you get to the real reason for the video. The biggest mistake that you can make is telling your viewers what they should be doing. They already understand that, that is why they are watching your video. Keep in mind that your viewer clicked on your video because they have a problem that they want to solve, or your title caught their attention. The best way to engage your viewers is by letting them know in the first 20 seconds or less what they are going to learn if they continue watching. It is critical that you do this in less than 20 seconds or your chances of losing a viewer is extremely high, so reel them in, hook them and reassure them that your video will solve their problem.

It is great idea to have your logo incorporated into your intro. There are a few ways that you can do this.

1. Have a custom intro made by a professional that normally cost a few hundred dollars.
2. You can design one yourself if you have the knowledge and tools to do so.
3. You can go to videohive.net and find a template in the logo strings section. Once you have your template you can hire an editor on Fiverr.com to customize your template with your logo and brand colors. This is the most cost-effective and runs for $50 or less.

The cornerstone to great marketing is delivering a message that your audience can relate to. Think about what you are good at and what information you want to share with your audience. The more valuable the information, the more they will trust you so do not be afraid to share what you know by thinking that you are giving away your stuff. When deciding on your video content decide what problem you will be solving, what you want to teach them, what you want to say, how you want to offer it and what your overall goal is for loading the material. When delivering your content be very direct and stay on track. Do not ramble and you don't need to go into detail for every little step, doing so may overwhelm and confuse your viewers.

When creating a "How to" video try to break up your steps as best as you can so that it is easier for your viewers to follow along. The ideal length for a video like this is 3-6 minutes, however it is totally ok to go over 6 minutes if it takes you that long to explain your steps in a way that your audience understands.

Before the close of your video make sure to encourage your viewers to head over to your website and one way to do this is by offering them a freebie on the same topic that your video is on or something that will help solve an additional problem for them. Consistency is key when deciding to use this platform. The more videos that you upload the more subscribers you will obtain. Your thumbnails are a very important element to catching the eye of your viewers. You do not have to be a professional at design to create a thumbnail is appealing. A free online site that I use is Canva. If you can not come up with anything creative check out some of your favorite YouTube channels and pay special attention to what their thumbnails look like. If all else fails, you can use a plain colored background and just add text.

The reason you created a YouTube channel in the first place is to build your business, right? The best to do this is by creating a call to action or freebie at the end of each and every one of your videos. You can do this by following the RPS (RECAP, PROBLEM, SOLUTION) formula. In 5-10 seconds, recap what you just taught them in your video. Example: "Alright, those are the 5 steps you need to make the perfect sugar cookie." Then continue by addressing an additional problem that will create demand for the freebie that you are offering. Example: "Now, you need the perfect ingredients to make your cookies taste great." Your solution will be to offer them your freebie that is related to the topic of your video. Then tell them how to obtain it. Example: "I've created a list of the exact ingredients that you need. Just click the link below to access the free recipe instantly."

To take your video marketing a step further, cut it into smaller clips and post it on Facebook and Instagram with links leading back to the full video. When posting your video to Instagram make sure to include the link to your full video in your Bio. You can also opt to pay for a post boost on either platform but before you do that make sure to read the Facebook section in this book where I explain the correct way to post an ad and receive great results. If you have an email list, it would be wise to shoot them an email advising them of your new video and providing the direct link. This allows you to get a high volume of viewers streaming from your email subscribers, Instagram and Facebook audience and an additional bonus will be for your video to get a boost in YouTube search results due to the rise in views. I recently learned about the search result boost after a few of my videos went viral and received over 10k views. After posting a clip-on Facebook, I suggest following up a week later and posting the full video.

There is a secret weapon that most people do not know about. Use this link: youtube.com/subscription center? add user=(YOURUSERNAME) every time you share your videos to another social media platforms. It will create an automatic pop-up that forces people to subscribe before they can watch the video that you posted, it's a foolproof way to increase your subscribers. The gag is that you must have a custom URL, which YouTube will provide for free once you have over 100 subscribers. Another useful tool that will make a significant difference in sending subscribes to your channel is adding keywords to your profile. You can do this by going to your creator studio, channel and then under advanced. You should see the box from there to add keywords that will make your channel easier for your target audience to find.

Webinars are awesome idea because they are full of tips and information. They are typically more than 30 minutes long and feels exclusive for people. If you want to do a webinar, what topic should it be on? Personally, it should be on a topic that resonates high with your audience. Maybe you have a lot of shares on a particular post. You can turn that into a webinar. Remember, not every follower or subscriber reads every post. You can totally repurpose that blog post into a webinar. Most webinars use slides to share their topic. You can use Keynote if you are a Mac user like me or use Google Slides to create your slides. If you are ready to do a webinar, you can do it for free with YouTube Live. Once you sign into YouTube, go to *Creator Studio* (click on your pic at the right-hand corner). On the sidebar click on *live streaming*. Click on *Events* and *Schedule a new event*.

Make sure to:

- Set your webinar to unlisted under *Public* setting (this makes it private and only those with the link will get to see your webinar)
- Click on *Quick (using Google Hangouts on Air)* setting

When you create your event, click on it and it will show you on YouTube. Click on the Share and you can use that link to tell your subscribers. What's nice is that link is the same before, during and after your webinar making it easy for people to watch the replay. Once it's time for the webinar, log in to your account and click on *Start Hangouts on Air*.

You can start 10 minutes earlier to make sure everything is working. People will come to your webinar when you tell them the time and click on your link.

Brand your channel, you only get one chance to make a good first impression. The best way to do that is by having a quality and professional icon picture of yourself and your header photo must be on point, its your prime real estate. For brand consistency your photos should match those that you use for your other social media accounts. Include your watermark logo on all your videos, you can do that by going to your creation studio, upload your logo and choose when you want it displayed in your video. The three options are at the beginning, during the entire video or at the end.

Your about tab should not be neglected, keep it short and sweet telling your audience who you are, what problem you can solve for them and why they should subscribe to your channel. When subscribers stay on your channel for long periods of time it increases your watch time, which let's google know that you have good content and will receive a higher ranking in the search. What's an easy way to do that? Playlist! If you are using the correct keywords in your titles, then your entire playlist can rank high in the search for those particular keywords and increase your channel optimization.

Adding featured channels is a great way to collaborate with other YouTubers. This is called cross promotion and by adding their channel they may return the favor, driving traffic to each others channel. You can do this by clicking on your channel, customize channel, and on the right-hand side there will be a box that says featured channels, click add channels and start adding your channels. If you have friends on YouTube that wish to increase their traffic, I may be beneficial to ask them to add your profile as one of their featured channels.

Make sure you are sending your subscribers to your conversion site, the place where they will potentially become a client or customer. A conversion site consists of a website, lead page, landing page or your shop page. Applying as a YouTube partner will also gain you access to adding your social links to the top of your channel. It is very easy to apply and takes a few days to be confirmed, however you will need 1k subscribers to be eligible. A little trick that a lot of people use to gain YouTube subscribers is by joining YouTube groups on Facebook and asking members for a Sub4Sub. This means you both subscribe to each other's channels.

Do you have a channel trailer? If not, create one ASAP. A channel trailer is a way to introduce yourself to new visitors and immediately lets them know why they should subscribe. Your channel trailer should include who you are, why you are credible (you're the CEO of _____, an author, or you're the creator of _____. How your channel will benefit your subscribers and a call to action. If you are a business owner, you should include your location and products or services that your offer in your trailers title. For examples go to YouTube and search channel trailers but for now I will tell you how to add your trailer. Its very simple and only consist of two steps. First go to my channel, click on customize channel and under the home tab the first column will say for returning subscribers and for new visitors. Click on each one and add which ever video you choose for your viewers to see once they land in your channel.

Let's talk about thumbnails for a moment. When you customize your thumbnails, it helps you stand out and acts as an extension of your brand. They should be consistent in color, font and should align with your branding identity. To add custom thumbnails, go to creator studio, next to the video that you want to change, click edit, choose a thumbnail from the ones that are prepicked for you or you have the option to upload your own, make sure to save your changes.

Linking your channel to your blog or website will also increase your visibility. I recently was on GoPro website and noticed that they link their social media channels at the bottom of every page on their website and have included a YouTube widget in their sidebar that shows their most recent video. You also have the option to go into your channel settings and adding auto-publish to twitter. Therefore, any video you upload will automatically get posted on twitter, unfortunately they do not have all of the main social sites available for auto publish but this may change in the future. Another easy step that you may find helpful is adding elements to the end of your video. There are only a few different options but basically, you're just reminding your viewer to subscribe, like your video and directing them to more of your content. You can do this by adding a subscribe button and a thumbnail of your next video. By clicking on your next video, you are boosting your watch time for your channel.

For business owners or bloggers some great content ideas may be to interview someone whom you consider important, how-to-videos, virtual tours or behind the scenes clips. You can record your computer screen while you show your audience how to do something in your area of expertise with a free screen capturing program called Camstudio. Narrating someone else's video has become really poplar especially for the gamers, or you can make a PowerPoint with slides of pictures or clip and narrate your reaction to each one.

Remember you are creating content to engage with your audience and to find new clients. I remember when I first started offering coaching services, I received a huge amount of new leads from my channel. My viewers watched me talk about business, share business and life tips and they loved my overall style. By this time, they knew who I was and what I had to offer them which lead to them being comfortable with purchasing from me. You can use your videos as a way to position yourself as an expert by sharing tips and tutorials within your niche, letting people know that you know what you are talking about.

Make sure to spread your videos across all your social media platforms, incorporate it into your blog post and send it to your email list in your weekly newsletter. You can create a video letting your audience know about an E-course which you can offer for free or charge and in your description leave the link where they can sign up.

If you need to ease your way in being live on camera you can start with creating some videos with just audio and graphics. When you first start taping live videos, you are going to be nervous and you probably wont like how you look or sound, upload it anyway. After a few videos you will begin to get comfortable in front of the camera and talking to yourself will become easier 😜□😜□😜□

Your video skills will improve so do not worry yourself with how many times you fumble your words or hair that is out of place because the more you practice the more you will improve, and you can always edit parts out of your video. Use your YouTube Live to your advantage. You can get familiar with being in front of the camera and hold a Q&A for your audience at the same time or if you are comfortable in front of the camera you can host live webinars, which will set you apart from other youtubers in your niche.

EQUIPMENT & LIGHTING

Natural light is the best light and looks amazing on video, for that reason I choose to film majority of my videos during midday. If you can not find a good spot with some natural light you need to make sure that your setup has white lighting pointing towards you. Try to avoid overhead and backlighting as much as you possibly can. Your microphone does not have to be expensive, in fact I purchased my mic with stand for under $40 bucks and if all else fails headphones with a mic will get you through.

For filming you can use a webcam, your iPhone or you can purchase a camera with great specs for video recording. Purchasing a video camera with the microphone already attached is also an option and may save you a few bucks. A really easy and FREE way to edit your videos is by using windows movie maker where you can add graphics, music and effects. If you are a little more advanced than Imovie or SocialBoxTV is the software that the professional Vloggers use. My all-time fav is Adobe Spark. This is a free online program that you do not have to download, and it is literally like a Canva on steroids. Check it out. To create screen capture videos, I like to use a software called Camtasia. Camtasia allows you to capture what you are doing on your computer screen and records your voice at the same time. Some free alternatives are Jing, CamStudio or ScreenFlow for Mac users.

To add music to your videos you will need royalty free music that will not get a copyright notice thrown at you. Here I've complied a list of free sites that you can grab music from with no worries. Your YouTube audio library would be the obvious choice, it is easy to use, and the songs are sorted my categories to help you find what you are looking for. Another popular site is Vimeo. To find the free songs click the advanced filter and change the search field to "Creative Commons-Attribution only" and you also have the option to select instrument only for background music with not vocals. For royalty free music that you can download without creating an account head over to Free Music Archive. Sound Gator is a hosting site that specializes in sound effects, so if you need a certain noise or effect this is your go to site. You will however need to create an account to download files. Bensound has some tracks as well, however per their term agreement, you must give text credit to the creator. Sounds Crate lets you download up to 5 free songs per day and you have the option to download a file in WAV which is a higher quality. And last but not least Pond5 has tons of royalty free music but it is a bit trickier to retrieve the files. Once you are on the site click on the music category. At the bottom click public domain music, select the track that you want and add it to your cart, it should say $0. To download you will need to create an account.

Take time at least once a week to read though your comments, answer questions and delete any rude comments. Just like any other platform there are not so nice people who will leaving weird comments. Keep it professional and just delete and block them.

With YouTube you can show your face and be more personable with your viewers and it opens up a new way to share your brands content. It can do great things for your business. If you use these strategies you will indeed have a super successful YouTube channel, just remember to be patient, and consistent with your content. The more consistent that you are the better your chances of building a loyal audience. Try to upload a new video at least once a week, anymore than that is a bonus!

<u>YOUTUBE CHECKLIST</u>

1. **Do you have a professional cover photo?**
2. **Is your profile photo professional?**
3. **Did you complete your About section?**
4. **Did you use plenty of keywords in your descriptions?**
5. **Is your website listed?**
6. **Do you have a video trailer?**
7. **Are you posting regularly?**
8. **Did you set up your playlist?**
9. **Did you subscribe to other channels?**
10. **Have you connected your other social media accounts?**
11. **Are you sharing your content?**
12. **Did you use Tags?**

INSTAGRAM

In record time Instagram has been able to absolutely explode into one of the most popular and frequently visited social media platforms of the planet. It is all about showing off a way of life and using glamorous looking pictures to make your products and services incredibly desirable. The truth is that Instagram is an incredibly powerful tool, a highly nuanced platform and something that deserves a big place in every single internet marketing campaign. It is about finding art in everyday activities. It's about taking something that is relatively dull and making it seem incredibly exciting.

Even before being purchased by Facebook, Instagram had hundreds of millions of users logging in, posting content and interacting with content every single day. On top of that Instagram was able to cultivate a truly active social media network in a way that many other social sites hadn't been able to. We are talking about game changing stuff here, especially when it comes to marketing and advertising. It is also the best platform for reaching women, so if you have products or services geared toward women, you definitely need to be utilizing this app. Honestly, you'd have to be a little bit crazy not to leverage everything that Instagram has to offer as far as building your business online. It is the key to numerous online marketing empires, and it can be an effective tool to help you build your business and the financial future you've always dreamed. Let's be honest, if you are a business owner you are not gramming for the fun of it, you're in it to make a profit as well. Well at least you should be.

A survey conducted by Iconosquare in revealed that 70% of users have at some point sought out a brand to follow on Instagram. 62% have followed brands they love and 41% are open to marketing messages and discounts. 65% of users also reported that they found it flattering when a brand liked their post. For personal brands the great thing is that people become fans of you and not just the product or service that you're promoting. From there, it is then your job to demonstrate that you 'live what you preach'. Your personal brand and your lifestyle match what your product is about.

So, if you have a blog about fitness and you have a personal brand, then your posts can be of you working out, of you eating healthy meals, of you going on healthy walks... etc. But the difference here is that you're also going to occasionally include photos that are more related to your personal life: maybe photos of you out and about with your friends, or photos of your other hobbies or your dog. If you get this right and if you've built enough of a relationship with your followers, then they will like getting these insights into your life and they will all become part of your image. Note that a personal brand works very well for Instagram Stories which have that very personal and intimate feel.

First, make sure your profile is PUBLIC, not PRIVATE. You can change this in Options -> Public/Private switch. This gets more people to see your posts because they can appear on the Discover page. Next, ask yourself if your username is recognizable. If you can't make your username to be the name of your business, at least use your business name in the first half of your username. This makes finding your page in searches way easier. Also, make sure that you add your full business name in Options -> Name. Make sure that your profile picture shows your brand logo. This will also help people recognize your page in searches. And finally, make sure that your bio is filled with creative and informative info about you and your business.

You must be smart and savvy about how you go about making the most out of Instagram. Because it is so simple to get started, it can lure people into being kind of lazy with their marketing and strategies. Use the inside information that I am about to share with you to not only jumpstart your Instagram marketing but also build the kind of business and brand on this platform that will set you up for unbelievable success moving forward.

In this chapter some of the things we'll cover include...

- A rundown of Instagram's features and history
- How to create stunning images and photos that really grab attention
- How to build and grow your audience to incredible heights
- How to ensure maximum engagement
- How to drive sales and downloads from your account
- How to use live video and Instagram Stories in order to create an even more powerful relationship with your viewers
- How to monetize your Instagram account
- How to integrate Instagram with your other social media activities and internet marketing strategies
- How to attract and acquire sponsors to earn a living solely from Instagram
- And much more!

KNOW YOUR TARGET MARKET

This is a step that majority of people marketing on Instagram ignore completely and is the final nail in their coffin before they even get started. You can not have real success with online marketing without first understanding exactly what's happening in your market, what your ideal client/customer is interested in, the kind of content that they gravitate to and the "hot buttons" that compel them to go from engaged follower to a paying customer. Don't make the mistake of trying to be everything to everyone, focus on your target audience and the people whom are actually looking for what you have to offer.

For starters, you must get crystal clear about who your ideal prospect really is. Sure, it isn't as sexy as leveraging the latest Instagram marketing tactic du jour, but it is the heart and soul of a proven marketing approach and the only way that you are going to be able to hit the ground running with your new Instagram advertising efforts.

A lot of business owners try to create their business and brand around what they are most interested in and feel as though "they" are the best customer for their products or services. These kinds of business owners are going to color all their marketing and advertising according to what they would be most attracted to, as opposed to what their customer would be interested in. Do not make this mistake.

Create a customer profile that is as detailed as humanly possible about whom your perfect prospect is. Break down their age, interest, hobbies that they most enjoy, their income, martial status, and everything else that you can come up with to really zero in on exactly who they are. Once you understand exactly who your perfect prospect is and what they want from your Instagram account most, it will become effortless to create the kind of Instagram content that will really resonate with them as a core individual.

By doing this you will be able to knock your marketing out of the park, turn the heat up and have an unfair advantage over your competitors. Speaking of your competitors......

CHECK OUT YOUR COMPETITION

It is impossible for you to have any measure of success on Instagram without first understanding what the lay of the land is like and what your competitors are doing that you have to do better. YOU MUST STAND OUT! Take time to check out the top 20 Instagram accounts in your industry and figure out what they are doing effectively. There is absolutely no reason whatsoever for you for jump in and reinvent the wheel when it comes to online marketing. Study what your competitors are doing and put your own twist to it. By paying attention to the content that they publish and how their followers respond will give you a head start without doing the heavy lifting. You will also be able to measure how frequently they post and whether this has an impact on how their followers engage. This will help you slip right into the top tier of Instagram accounts in your industry when you're publishing the same type of content that the "big dogs" are.

Some businesses are able to hit it right off the bat with daily or weekly post, but if your competitor is publishing content on a weekly basis, you may be able to squeeze right in and capture a larger audience by ramping up the speed in which you put out new content. This is where real savvy marketers are able to turn Instagram traffic into cold hard cash and something that you are going to have to master as quickly as possible.

More importantly by paying attention to your competition you are also going to be able to find new collaborations that may help you skyrocket your success. By looking at your competitors and finding the kind of content that they are interested in sharing and that your market is most interested in as well, can give you the opportunity to reach out to them and offer to provide some content to them in exchange for a "mention". You can then piggyback off the following that they already have developed and jumpstart your success.

It's really all about finding leverage and squeezing every single drop out of every Instagram post that you make. You can not just throw content on Instagram in a willy-nilly kind of fashion and expect to have any real success. It just isn't going to happen that way. Peeping out your competition will give you tremendous insight into what they are doing successfully and what they are doing unsuccessfully so that you can avoid that pitfall and pivot it into a competitive advantage. It really doesn't get much better than that!

CONSISTENCY IS KING

To reach out and connect with your target market on Instagram you have to reach out to them effectively, consistently and reliably. One study shows that Instagram marketing is only impactful and influential after someone sees your content on seven separate occasions and that you must make sure that every single piece of content you publish is integrated with your brand so that it is immediately recognized as you.

You also must make sure that you post your content on a regular and consistent basis so that your followers know when to expect new post from you. This means you want to post at least once a day (or every other day, or twice a day, find what fits your needs best) and try to keep it around the same time daily. Think about how difficult it would be for you to follow up with your favorite TV show if it was on Wednesday one week, Sunday the next, and then went on a three-week hiatus until it returned on Monday night and then Tuesday night the next week.

Sure, you may be able to capture the attention of some "channel flippers" on Instagram but you're never going to be able to build up the kind of consistent and engaged following that you want without sticking to an obvious schedule. All of the biggest companies on the planet have and stick religiously to marketing calendars for this very reason. Not only does it allow them to plan out their marketing and content months in advance, but it also allows them to communicate consistently with their followers in a way that they understand and relates to. This kind of consistency creates a real relationship with your market.

Trust me, building out that content calendar is essential if your going to systemize your business and have any real chance at incredible success in Instagram marketing and turning complete strangers into fanatical returning customers.

By engaging with your followers and sending them to your other social media platforms, you increase the strength of the relationship. This is definitely going to transfer into better influence and a greater opportunity of converting them into paying customers.

INSTAGRAM STORIES & VIDEO FUNCTION

Instagram stories can essentially be summed up as Instagram's attempt to jump on the SnapChat gravy train. This might seem like a small or unexciting new feature for the platform, but it represents a bold step into the future for Instagram and a massive opportunity for marketers. Imagine the benefit as a product manufacturer of being able to demo your product live on air and then answer questions about it in real time.

Stories are a new way to communicate with your audience is a more direct and immediate way which will help you increase engagement with your audience. It makes them feel as though you are talking directly to them or as thought they are being bring along for the ride and are there with you. Making your followers feel as though they are getting to know you is a great way to increase trust and brand loyalty.

Stories are a great way to show behind the scenes and the day to day aspects of your business. Using Instagram stories allows you to be more visible and show more of your brand. The best part is that it gives your brand a face and you don't have to think about a caption or worry whether your post aligns with your brand colors. Another thing to keep in mind about Instagram Stories is that they will appear right at the top of your viewers feed, thereby ensuring that they will be much more likely to see it.

Video content, live videos and boomerangs (short repeating videos much like GIFs) has increasingly become very popular on social media and thus it is of paramount advantage for anyone looking to market in a creative manner to visually communicate with their followers, customers and fans. First there was Periscope, then came Facebook Live now we are seeing live video on Instagram too. There is good reason for this. Live video is one of the biggest and most important innovations in social media so far and is one of the best tools that marketers have at their disposal for engaging with their audience. Putting a face to your brand helps build trust with your followers. People buy from people that they trust, and the Instagram video feature will help you create that emotional connection with your audience. You can invite your viewers along to join in on your workouts, to attend events with you or to join you over your morning bowl of cereal. Whatever the case, you will be able to directly engage with your followers while your audience is able to share in on a ton of different experiences with you.

The significant thing here is that this function allows one to share their day to day experience in a casual and informal way giving followers and customers a feel for your business and you as a person. Sharing behind the scenes activities has been noted to rank well on Instagram, particularly if it is from a service provider. Such videos make your company more trustworthy and attractive which in turn positively affects one's exposure and visibility. It gives you a chance to show off what you are offering. One of the best things about Instagram live is that it will allow you to see comments posted live on your videos as you are filming them. That means that you can then respond to those comments instantly and your audience can feel as though they are talking to you directly. Imagine how much this can improve your engagement and trust you're your viewers when they feel that you are a real person that they can communicate with directly. Simply tap the plus symbol at the top of your Instagram account to open up your Stories and then select Live. Embrace the video and stories function and be rewarded.

Want to create some behind the scenes stories? Here are some ideas. Show your followers your office space, make some boomerangs of your morning cup of coffee, ask your followers if they prefer coffee or tea in the morning, create a story of your packaging or shipping process, film yourself unpacking products that you have gotten delivered, show your audience what you are working on, and you can also show them what went wrong on a product, everything doesn't have to be all glitter and glam.

Fun fact Friday is something that you can do on a regular basis. You could share a fun fact about yourself, the people you work with or just a random fact that you can find on the internet to share on Fridays. You can show your product being used or create a how to story teaching something on the topic of your choice. A live Q&A can be very engaging or if you attend an event let your viewers know what you are learning and how you plan to implement it into your business.

Hashtag stickers can get more exposure to your stories if you want to improve your brand awareness. You can also hide the sticker. Maybe your strategy is to attract more local customers to your business, but you do not want the sticker to show. You can make a sticker with your city and exact location and hide it by clicking on it and making it smaller with your fingers until you can not longer see it. When using hashtags, you want to make sure that you are connecting with other people who are using that hashtag. By doing so they make check out your account and become a customer. The more you interact on Instagram, the higher your chances of converting a follower into a customer.

Creating story highlights to showcase your products or services can easily turn your followers into customers. You can talk about your services or show the quality of your product in creative ways using your highlights. You may show your summer or fall collections if you are a boutique owner or bloggers can showcase their latest blog posts. You can utilize apps like hype type to animate your stories or pic collage to create polls or to show multiple pictures of your new products at once.

The overall aim is to inspire and sell the dream. You want to focus on a single value proposition and promote a specific lifestyle. Ask yourself: what is the value proposition of your business and how can you portray that in a visual way? Your value proposition is your 'dream'. It's the dream that people are willing to pay money for and it's the dream that will set your business apart from the competition. The dream is what will turn followers into true fans and what will get you likes and shares and follows. And Instagram is all about selling dreams. Some of the most productive and lucrative accounts on Instagram are pages that focus on fitness, fashion, food, travel and Pc gaming.

One thing to always remember is before posting anything ask yourself would you be happy with that content being the first impression that a visitor has of you and your brand? If the answer is no, then perhaps it is better suited for your personal page or just shared threw a text message with friends.

To get started...

1. First, right click on the plus icon that is found at the top left of the home screen. This will be next to the other stories and it will say 'My Story' next to it with your profile images. You can also click on the Instagram icon above and to the left, depending on your version and your region. You can also launch this by just swiping left from the main feed, or by swiping right from the home screen.

2. Now tap the circle button that is found at the bottom of the screen in order to take a photo. Or you can tap and hold if you want to record a video.

3. From there, you can then edit the photos or videos as you normally would in Instagram, or you can draw or write on the screen just like you would if you were using Snapchat (there are a LOT of similarities here in fact...). To add filters, you simply swipe across it and there will be seven to pick from (less than usual, though we suspect more are on the way).

4. Badges again work like Snapchat and allow for a little more editing in your images. A cool trick that some Instagram creators are using is to use the polka dot image in order to create thought bubble effects.

5. You can also tag people in your stories using the @symbol as you normally would. They will be alerted in Instagram direct and can then check out the story.

6. Tap 'Done' to save your story and then tap the check-mark button the share it.

Each time you add a new photo, it will be added to your story and your fans will be able to watch those images and videos in a slideshow. Remember: your stories will appear at the top of the home feed and will be indicated by a red ring circling your profile picture. Users who want to view your stories can then click on that image and will be able to sit back and watch the slide show, or swipe through images in order to speed it along.

If you want to go live, then this will work just a little bit differently. All you need to do is open up the stories camera by swiping or clicking the plus button and then select the 'Live' option. This is found along the bottom next to the 'Normal' and 'Boomerang' options. A live tag will now appear on your Instagram Stories bubble, so that followers will know that they can tap it in order to see what you're doing live. Something else neat about going live is that your followers will be notified even when they're not on Instagram (unless they have actively turned this off). This increases engagement and it's a great way to get people to join in with whatever you're doing and to increase engagement.

At any time, you can click to rotate the camera and if you select the 'Hands Free' option, then you'll be able to record without holding down the button. This is useful for recording workouts or other things where you want to be in the shot and not talking directly to the camera. You'll also be able to see people appearing and disappearing in the live video and this is a good way to get more engagement – when you see someone join your chat, why not welcome them and ask them how they are?

Stories and live videos are crucial when it comes to selling. Someone is going to be much more likely to want to buy from you once they feel as though they know you – when they've seen just how your ideas and services have helped you in your own life and once, they've seen you playing with your dog or celebrating Christmas with your family.

Certain content works particularly well for Stories or being live videos. Here are some suggestions:

Stories

- Photos with fans are great for stories
- Behind the scenes photos also work very well for stories and can be a great way to build anticipation for something. Got a new video in the works? Then why not post a photo of you filming or editing the video? Product development, store renovation, employees at work or a team meeting.
- Sequential photos – seeing as stories work like a slideshow, there are some fun affects you can pull off by uploading a few photos in a sequence. How about a few photos that show something you're cooking getting created?
- Photos that wouldn't be particularly attractive but that nevertheless fit your brand also work.
- You can also add photos that supplement the other photos you've taken. For instance, if you have taken 10 photos of the same activity, then you won't want to flood your account with them. Choose one or two for your grid and add the rest to your story.
- Stories are also a great place to shout out to another creator if you want to do a cross promotion!
- Jokes and funny memes also work great here!

Live Videos

- Travels – If you're travelling and you've come across something amazing, then why not let your followers come along with you for the ride?
- Events – The same goes for events. Bring your viewers to concerts, to premieres and to any other exciting events you might attend. In this case, video will let your viewers almost experience that lifestyle you're promoting!
- Interviews – Let your visitors actually ask you questions and interact with you! Or how about conducting an interview with another person and letting your viewers take part in that?

46

- Reviews and showcases – Got a product to promote? Why not showcase it live?
- Workouts
- Vlogs and discussions

WHY CAPTIONS MATTER

They create a relationship with your potential customers. Have you ever made a friend without having a conversation with them first? Probably not. Conversation is that start of any relationship and in order to gain you customers trust you must engage with them. Communicating with your followers will give you the opportunity to learn their likes and dislikes, what catches their attention, get their opinions on things and you can give them some free tips and advice. Remember it takes a lot more effort to comment on a post whether than just like it, that means they are interested in your content. Comments are like algorithm gold and shows Instagram that your content is attracting attention, which in turn will lead them to pushing your content in more feeds, potentially being ranked in the top post section or getting recommended on the explore tab. Think about this with every post that you share to your followers, you want to show up and create captions that make people want to carry on the conversation further.

Instagram does not have a share button like Facebook, therefore you must write personality filled captions that your audience can relate to. You wouldn't tag your friends to a dull post but if the caption resonates with you, you are tagging your friend like "Omg Tasha this is so us" ......when someone tags their friends to your post that is generating more exposure to your brand. Show your personality and connect on a personal level so that your followers get to know you as a person. They will begin to remember your name, your favorite things and your habits. Sell your story not your products or services. Give them something to remember and get them excited to buy and support you. Make a name for yourself so when they don't see you on their feed for awhile or are looking for the product that you offer, they can come searching for you.

Your followers want to connect with like minded individuals, have their thoughts and opinions heard, share advice, follow accounts that they can relate to and that are interactive, want to laugh, learn and be encouraged. Are your captions serving any of those purposes? To write better captions read them out loud before hitting the share button, does it sound like you, do you use these phrases in real life? When you present yourself as just being you, you will attract the type of customer that you want, the type that loves you and your brand. Let your brand tell a story that your customers can see within themselves.

Don't get me wrong, sharing your sales and products are allowed. Your audience knows that you are a business and expect to see advertisements. However, you must be creative in presenting it in a helpful and encouraging way. Give them direction by giving them a call to action, let them know what you want them to do next, don't assume that they automatically know. This could be simply instructing them to tag their friends, click the link in your bio or to double tap the photo. You get to decide how you want to present your business, how you interact with your audience and what things you share with your followers. So how will you stand apart from your competitors? What do you want to be known for?

Make sure you are sharing in your captions how you are using your own products or services. If you have a book on how to get fit, then it will sell much better when people realize that it contains the secrets that you followed in order to get the incredible body and enjoy the incredible workouts that you have been showcasing on your channel for so long.

RUNNING CONTESTS WORKS WONDERS

A great approach to growing your account quickly is to run regular contest where you actually give away quality items or services in exchange for increased follower numbers and exposure. This is a proven, tried and true effective marketing tactic that has been in use long before Instagram was even thought of. The only thing that you must do is fulfill your end of the deal by providing the products or services that you promised. It may cost you a little bit upfront but when you actively monetize your Instagram account, you'll find that the return on investment is well worth it.

Contest are one of the proven ways to gain insta-traction, which gives you a chance to be openly creative with your marketing. There are different types of contest that you can run such as like contest, which involves uploading a photo and asking your audience to like it for a chance to win. This type of competition increases your chances of appearing on the Discover page and it is one of the simplest ways to increase traction. If the primary goal is to generate feedback about your products or services and increase post engagement, comment contests are the way to go. Simply upload a photo and ask your followers to comment on the post for a chance to win a prize and always ask your followers to tag other users. Photo contest is when you tell users to post a photo on their personal accounts and use a hashtag of your choice-this will help you find the post to pick a winner. This type of contest can also include asking your followers to repost one of your posts for a chance to win.

The purpose of contest is to draw in the right followers and the best way to find those users is by offering giveaways that are relevant to your brand. Simply give the rules in your caption section or provide a link to your website in your bio that provides all of the rules of getting to win the contest.

It all comes down to getting the word out about your contest. Hashtags are the best way to spread the word as well as track entries. Take a look at the accounts of leading businesses in your niche (a niche of course is a subject matter and it can also mean your industry) and note the type of hashtags they are using. The right combination of hashtags will boost the exposure of our contest, bringing in more traction.

At the end of the day, new followers are not cold hard cash in the bank unless you actually begin to monetize your followers and your account. Having a big Instagram following can be very lucrative for marketing and driving traffic to your page, however its more than a simple numbers game. Simply having a huge following doesn't necessarily mean anything, the key is having active followers-people who not only follow you but actively like and comment on your post. These are the people that you want to target when growing your audience.

The easiest way to monetize your account is simply to use content as an entry level to your marketing funnel. You'll be able to push visitors deeper in your funnel by putting out interactive marketing material, therefore converting at least some of them into paying customers.

For many people, finding a sponsor on Instagram is the ideal way to make a living. Imagine being able to earn money by posting photos of yourself working out, using products you've been sent or just looking great in free clothes. Finding sponsors on Instagram means that brands will pay you to post pictures wearing their clothes, drinking from their protein shakers, or working on their computers. You can get free stuff this way as well as make some extra income. In short, you will be able to make money by doing the things you love and even getting moderately famous for it! That's an amazing dream but how can you make it a reality? Here are some tips that can help…

The first thing to identify is how creators get in touch with sponsors in the first place. The answer is that this can happen one of two ways: either the sponsors find you and get in touch, or you find them and ask if they want to sponsor you. You can find sponsors by heading over to Revfluence.com or Famebit.com… and there are many more sites just like this. If you can manage to grow your channel large enough, then you can rest assured that sponsors will get in touch and you don't need to worry about chasing them. The more followers that you have, the more you can charge these companies. You should also make sure that your brand is consistent – that you have a consistent theme and that you promote a positive message. You need to look professional and avoid slander or posting anything in poor taste. You need to represent the kind of brand that big companies are going to want to associate with. This is a pretty easy way to get paid for doing what you love, so all you need to concentrate on is getting big!

On the other hand, you can find sponsors by looking online at platforms designed to pair off creators and sponsors. Many of these websites exist and they're very easy to use. Of course, the more followers you have the better deals you will be qualified for. Once again, your priority is to grow your accounts.

Sponsors are always looking to find partners that are aligned with their goals. That is to say that they want to find people to work with who echo their principles and who have the same values. Therefore, it is so important to avoid controversy or being too off topic when posting your branding content. If you make a controversial statement and you are sponsored, that means that the sponsor is endorsing what you are saying. This is a quick way to halt big brands from working with you and it means that you will potentially miss out on opportunities moving forward.

It's also important to ensure that your message is consistent. Occasionally, your Instagram posts are likely to be 'off topic' and that is fine. Just try to make sure that for the most part, you stick with your niche whether that be fitness, fashion or music. When a sponsor checks out your channel, you want them to find a long list of excellent images, all highly related to the subject matter that they are wanting to promote. And of course, you also need to ensure that your photos are high quality and that they have a professional looking sheen. No one will want to associate with grainy, poorly composed photos!

HOW TO GROW YOUR ACCOUNT

The first thing you need to do to ensure that your Instagram account will grow quickly, is to post content consistently. That means you need to be consistent in terms of the frequency of your posting and in terms of the nature of the posting. People need to learn what they can expect from your account, so that they can make the decision whether to follow you.

If you created the personal brand as mentioned earlier, then it's okay to be a little bit looser in terms of what you post. But if you have a fitness brand and all you ever post are pictures of your dogs, then you're going to lose your followers. Likewise, if you have a productivity brand and you fill it with images of yourself travelling, you will lose fans. So be consistent and make sure that you are posting relevant content at least daily – ideally a lot more than that.

You also need to do whatever else you can do to help people know what your brand is all about. One of your most powerful tools in this respect will be your logo and your brand name. If you have an account all about fitness, then you need a logo and a name that will communicate this as soon as people see it. You want your first-time viewers to instantly know what you're all about so that they can decide if they want to follow you and if your content is for them.

One thing you can do right away to grow your Instagram account is to bring in visitors from your other channels. One simple way to do this is to add a button on your website that people can click in order to follow you on Instagram. One thing I have done for instance, is to add a feed from my Instagram into the right-hand column of my website. That way, everyone who visits my website will be able to see the kind of things I post on Instagram and then may decide to follow me. This way, the more people you bring to your website, the more you will be able to grow your Instagram account. This will then also work in reverse; so that as your Instagram account grows, you are able to send more and more people back to your website!

Use IFTTT (If This, Then That) in order to publish your Instagram pictures straight to your Twitter account. You should also be using the sharing buttons within Instagram to post your content to your other social media accounts. For example, you can set it up so that any new picture added to Instagram will automatically be posted to your Twitter account as well as your Facebook page. That way, people who aren't following you on Instagram will still be exposed to your content and they'll get taken straight to your Instagram account if they click the image.

This sounds a little too simplistic to be effective but ask people to follow you! One of the very best ways to get more people to follow you on Instagram is simply to ask them to go and check out your page. At the end of posts and YouTube videos, I'll say 'check out my Instagram account for more fashion inspiration' etc. This is a great way to draw attention to it and to make sure that it doesn't get overlooked.

One of the most powerful ways to massively explode your channel on Instagram is to use influencer marketing. This essentially means that you're going to contact someone who is already highly popular on Instagram and then you're going to try and convince them to promote you in some way. You might find a prominent fashion model and ask them if they would consider sharing one of your images or to promote your product in exchange for free items. That way, you gain instant access to a huge proportion of the people that they have access to. Don't go straight for the biggest creators on Instagram with a million followers or they likely won't answer you (they get a lot of messages). Instead, look for someone who is just a little bit bigger than you – someone that you can stand to gain from but that is still small enough that they might be flattered that you contacted them.

You should always be interacting with your Instagram community. When someone comments on your post, take the time to acknowledge that comment-like it and reply to them. Research shows that Instagram users find it flattering when brands like their pictures. And chances are that when they are flattered, they will want to check out exactly who it is that likes their photos! So, search for different tags and see what other people are contributing. If you post about fashion a lot, then how about searching for the tag 'fashion', seeing what other people have contributed and then leaving some comments on those posts. They'll check you out to see what you're all about and if they find a ton of amazing photos that appeal to them, chances are that they'll follow you! Try to commit to commenting on ten photos per day.

You will notice an increase in interaction over time if you take the initiative of talking to your followers. You should also be spending time every day scrolling through hashtags that are relevant to the information you share on Instagram. While you scroll through its important that you keep liking and commenting on post. What's the best way to draw people to your page? Show genuine appreciation for their page!

If you are looking to gain a large following quickly there is a fairly simple and straightforward strategy that you can follow that has proven itself time and time again. This requires that you find pages with large followings that are similar in content to yours. Go to their pages and follow their followers. Typically, you want to follow between 25-30 pages in a single session, then allow them some time to follow you back. If you want to increase your chances of getting a follow in return, you can like and comment on a few of their post when you follow them. After you have allowed some time for them to follow you, you will then unfollow everyone from that page that you followed before. Repeat this often and you will find that your followers will increase quickly with real, organic followers.

Part of your aim as an Instagram marketer, is to sell a dream. You want to promote a certain lifestyle and communicate a particular way of life that your audience will find inspiring and that will convince them to follow your channel and hopefully buy from you. If you have a fitness brand for instance, then you need to portray a lifestyle that's all about health and fitness and that makes you appear to be in amazing shape and to have everything going for yourself. If you have a clothing brand, then you need to post content of you looking beautiful and attractive thereby selling that dream. So, the question is... how do you go about selling the dream?

When it comes to painting a picture with your Instagram pictures, it's crucial that you pay attention to the small details. You need to communicate an image of being successful, organized, healthy and confident. No one wants to buy from someone who seems as though they can't get their own act together! And it's the tiny things you forget that can imply a lot about you. For example, if you are taking photos of technology to make it look desirable on Instagram, then you need to think about the condition of the item and think about the backdrop. Is the phone that you're showing off covered in dust? Because if so, then it's not going to look premium or desirable! Is there a coffee stain on the table? Because if so, it's going to make your home look untidy and therefore unprofessional! Even the weather matters. If you take a photo of someone outside in the sun, then that will look glossier and more professional than the very same photo taken in the rain. Of course, Instagram is all about the filters and this is one of the things that makes it so well suited to being used for marketing. A filter can increase the saturation and contrast in a photo, thereby making a sunny location look that much brighter and more vivid. Even if the viewers know it isn't true to life, it's all about the way it makes them feel. Other filters can make a photo more retro, or 'grungier'. Think about the emotions you want to evoke and tweak your photo to suit that!

Instagram is the second largest social media platform on the net and is one of the very best in terms of engagement. It has the ability to inspire like almost no other platform thanks to its highly visual nature. By using Instagram, you can make your products and services look more glamorous and exciting therefore selling a dream to your audience. But in order to do that, you're going to need to learn how to take great photos, its that simple. Instagram is an entirely visual medium and in order to sell your value proposition and to stand out as a top creator, you need photos that immediately grab attention and that look the part. Getting a camera phone that has a relatively high pixel count is one good way to do this. You can also benefit from a wide-angle lens and other features like manual focus for when you want to create macro effects (where the subject is in high definition, but the background appears blurred).

One important tip is that you always need to spend time constructing your shot and thinking about the details. In other words, it is not enough to simply point and shoot – you need to think about things like the angle of the lighting and the backdrop. All it takes is to notice the angle of the sun and to move around your subject to create a much more professional looking shot that will be more visually interesting. As a general rule, it is usually advisable to try and create 'Rembrandt lighting'. This means that the light will be shining on your subject from a right angle, thereby lighting one side and leaving the other side in relative shade. Use a window, or better yet: create lighting using a soft box or another accessory.

Also, you need to think about your backdrop. Make sure that the background is visually interesting without distracting from the subject. When choosing an angle and setting up your shot, you should think about the foreground, middle ground and background. This will create more depth and give your shots a feeling of being three dimensional. Ideally, there should be something of interest at every level, as well as elements that will lead the eye from the foreground and into the background (such as a path leading into the background or a river).

You can also consider scale: ask yourself how you can portray the relative sizes and speeds of different objects. If you want to show how big something is, make sure it is surrounded by smaller items for scale and it will have much more impact! What's also highly important is the lighting equipment and a well-lit photo is always going to look considerably more professional than a poorly lit one. A great way to get good lighting is with a 'softbox', which will enable you to increase the contrast in any photo without making it look overly bright. Try to light objects from the side for more interesting shadows and a more dramatic effect.

Another tip is to consider getting colored lighting, which you can achieve with bulbs from LifX or Hue. These can create some very attractive effects that will look great if you are taking photos of products – especially if you can place them onto a clean and somewhat reflective surface such as an oak desk. Something else to consider is the props, backdrops and other elements that you can bring into your photos. These don't have to cost a lot of money but a few of the right props can make your photos much more exciting!

Finally, try to avoid photos that simply show an object. Instead, think about the emotional impact of your images and how they can tell a story. For instance, you can tell a story by using 'clues' in your photos to suggest something that has previously happened or that is yet to happen. Footprints in the sand can show that you have been jogging and are a little more interesting than a simple photo of someone running! You can also create more drama or interest by choosing interesting, contrasting items that wouldn't normally be in photos together. Another tip is to change the angle of your photos, which can help you to present more dynamic and dramatic imagery. Having a photo taking from a lower angle for instance can make any subject appear larger and more imposing!

Instagram is a powerful marketing tool that is not only the second largest social media platform on the web but also one of the biggest in terms of user engagement. A photo can tell a thousand words and if you consistently post great quality images that promote a certain lifestyle or dream, then you can gain a massive and highly engaged following that will be highly eager to buy from you. In short, the key to success on Instagram is to tell stories, to sell a dream and to promote a lifestyle that people want to be a part of! Dive in and start telling *your* story!

FACEBOOK

Facebook is the largest and most popular of the social networking sites, and is currently growing at a phenomenal rate, as you probably have already discovered and is available in over 70 different languages. Unlike other social sites that people visit fleetingly, the average user visits Facebook four times a day and spends at least 30 minutes a day on the site. Facebook was originally founded in early 2004 by a group of ex-Harvard university students as a service that was initially restricted to students of their own university. From there, Facebook rapidly expanded their services into most of the Ivy League universities in the USA, and thereafter it went to a larger scale in the USA, spreading to most universities and eventually down into high schools as well. Next, the site went international by moving into Canada, Australia and the UK so that it was open to anyone who had a university or college e-mail address. In late 2006, Facebook finally took the decision to move away from these educational grassroots and became a truly open service that anybody, anywhere in the world could register with and participate in. To put Facebook's current rate of expansion into some kind of perspective, one year ago the site was enjoying 15,000 new user signups per day, with 350 million active users currently accessing Facebook from their mobile devices. The average user is connected to 80 community pages (Brand pages, groups, events) and more than 250 million photos are uploaded per day. Perhaps more interestingly, Zuckerberg also claims that the fastest growing demographic group of new Facebook users is in the over 25 years of age group.

Facebook is currently enjoying 70 billion-page views per month and is the sixth most trafficked website in the USA, having recently surpassed eBay, and is now rapidly closing in on Google's traffic figures. If you then add in the fact that Microsoft has recently paid 240 million US dollars for a 1.6% stake in Facebook (which values the company at around $80 billion in total) you clearly have a picture of a company and the website that is going places very quickly.

If your objective with Facebook is to promote a product or service, then you might want to feature links to your website in as many ways as possible to drive visitors from Facebook back to your website or blog. One way that you can advertise your business is by creating a new group and featuring your link to your website.

You may have noted from the top left-hand side bar of the homepage that there is a section of the Facebook site that is called 'Marketplace'. This is the Classified Advertising section of the Facebook site. It could be highly profitable to create a short classified and sending readers from there to your website or blog where you would promote your products and services. When doing this make sure that you are placing your advertisement in the place where it is most likely to be seen. Keep in mind that the primary objective of placing your ad is to drive people to your website or blog where you will be able to do a proper sales job and collect additional email addresses for later use. You may also consider placing an ad for products that are free of charge such as a short e-book or a downloadable product that you offer. Everyone likes to receive something free, so this strategy can almost guarantee increased clicks to your website.

Enhance the effectiveness of your ads by including attractive pictures wherever possible in order to make your ads stand out from the crowd. Finally, you will note that your classified advertisement can either be limited to your specific geographical location or be published on a worldwide basis. Of course, if you are selling a tangible, physical product that requires delivery, then it would probably make sense to limit the distribution of your ad. If, however, your product is digitally delivered, then there is no logical reason to limit the scope and therefore the reach and effectiveness of your ad will have a greater impact.

Create a page. Sounds simple, right? It is – the problem is marketers get confused and they start a profile instead of a page. If you want to market your business on Facebook, a profile simply won't cut it. Pages are meant for businesses and they are much more effective at getting your message out there. You want to make sure that you have a professional looking profile and cover photo. Your business profile picture can be kind of tricky because sometimes your logo may be good to use, however if you are the face of your brand in any way then you may want to use a professional and clear photo of yourself. People like to see real faces and it makes you more personable to your followers, also your profile picture should be the same across all of your social media platforms so that your fans recognize your brand. Try to use a photo that is memorable and creates strong branding. Your cover photo is the most important piece of real estate on your page and should represent your brand by staying with your color scheme and theme. It should capture your audience's attention and make them want to scroll your page. Some different cover options to try are sharing testimonies, showing off your product, announcing a contest, highlight an event or show social proof. Then you will promote your page. One way you can do this is by placing your page URL in your email signature. Now every time you send an email, it's another chance for recipients to find your Facebook fan page.

Customize the tabs on your page. If you are following me on Facebook, then you may have noticed that I have a YouTube and Pinterest tab linked to my page. This helps my followers stay connected to me across my other social platforms. In order to do this, you must go to your personal page and once there go to your search bar. Type in "YouTube Tab" or whichever platform that you want to link. It will take you to the apps area and you can choose which tab you want to use. Next you will be prompted to select which page you want to add the tab on. Follow the prompts and your all set.

Make sure that you are utilizing your call to action buttons that are located under your cover photo. There are thirteen to choose from. (Call now, Contact Us, Send Message, Sign Up, Get Quote, Send Email, See Offers, Join Group, Book

Now, Use App, Learn More, Shop Now, Watch Video) Pick the one that best suits your needs and customize it. This is a great free tool and it even gives you the analytics of how many clicks you receive. On your personal FB page, you want to make sure that you link your business page under the "work" section.

Next, blog about your fan page. Don't just ask your blog readers to like your page – instead, give them at least one compelling reason why they should. Now, add a "Like" option to your blog or websites that links back to your page. Second, Tweet about your page. Ask your Twitter followers to like your fan page. Again, offering them a good reason why they should like it will greatly increase your response rate. Give people a great reason to become your fan. Maybe it's to get discounts or updates. Maybe it's a free video, e-book, etc. Just make sure it's something that motivates immediate action.

Add your page URL to YouTube. Do you create videos to promote your business? Then by all means add your fan page URL link to your videos, either at the end of the video or at the beginning of the video description. Ask your fans to like your content so it gets shared on their walls. You can't ask every time, but now and then is fine. When they like your post, more people will see it, which can lead to more fans – always a good thing.

Post frequently. If you forget about your fan page, your fans will forget about you. Post once or twice a day with good info, updates and questions. Don't make it all about you and your products. Instead, post about events, news, your industry and so forth. And whenever you can, inject a little humor into the mix. Get your fans involved with your page by starting discussions about your products and services or industry news. What's the best way to start a discussion? Simply ask a provocative question your fans cannot ignore. If you get stuck on what to ask, use the fill in the blank kind of question, such as, "If you could have any job in the world, it would be _____." Puzzle pictures also create great engagement. Photo such as "How many can you find in the picture". Remember to use plenty of photos and even videos. Written words are great, but videos are better, and photos tend to get shared. So, incorporate a variety of mediums into your Facebook communications. Facebook is not the place for a suit and tie kind of personality. Instead, be fun, be casual, be funny and make your fan page an entertaining, inviting place to be.

If you want to grow your fan base and increase your likes, you are going to need to have posts to your page that are interesting and keep your visitors wanting to return. Here are 3 tips to create Facebook posts that are engaging.

#1 Use Copy, Images and Videos That Are Engaging

* Photos and videos that are media rich will get attention and they will help your message be more noticeable on a News feed.

* Lifestyle and inspirational images are always engaging. Smart Page owners are quick to take advantage of these images, because they understand they do not have to be relevant to the product/service you offer to be relevant to your fans. Fill in the blank, caption this photo and remember when post always tend to get great interaction because they are fun, and your follower will not be feeling like you are always trying to sale them something. These fans will then share these posts with their friends and that provides you with more reach and another opportunity to grow your 'Likes.'

* Share images/photos of your products with your customers and encourage your visitors to post pictures on your wall, which will help your Facebook page to show up in the News Feed. Facebook users love pictures, so take advantage of them and encourage your followers to openly share their photos.

#2 Share and Promote Discounts and Promotions That are Exclusive

* Offer your visitors a really good perk or deal to keep them interested. You can increase your sales and increase your followers with this technique.

* Buy 1 get 1 free seems to be a very popular promotion and when you are giving things away for free.

* To increase your visitors' engagement, make sure that you have a clear call to action.

#3 Suitability and Timeliness

* When your posts are related to what they are thinking about at the time, such as holidays or a current sporting event, your audience is much more likely to engage. I have also found that people interact more with educational and

inspiring post. How to guides and live videos are really popular right now and are great ways to interact with your fans and at the same time they get to see your personality which will build trust and ultimately lead to increased sales.

* Timeliness in replying to any posts that have a comment on them is also important. The faster you are to reply to your fans the more likely that they will continue to engage you.

Do not become a troll victim. Now that you're starting discussions, remember to remain professional at ALL TIMES, with no exceptions. If you are perceived as quarreling with a fan, it won't matter if you're right – it will only matter that you lost your cool and you look really unprofessional. And if things look like they may get nasty, offer the fan a private way to contact you (phone or email, for example.)

Forget the "I" and focus on the "we." Much like writing a sales letter, making Facebook posts should be all about "we," not I. For example, "We reached 500 likes today, thank you everyone!" Be thankful. This one takes a little time, but it's well worth it. Thank each new person who likes your Facebook page or give a mention/tag to someone who has recently purchased your product. This will really make you stand apart from the crowd. After all, how many people have ever personally thanked them for a Like? You might very well be the first.

Brand your page. That large image on your timeline needs to ROCK. It should effectively communication the message you want to send to your fans, so spend some time getting it just right. Use Facebook insights to discover when people are most engaged with your content. This way you know when to post to get the maximum effect. And encourage people to return to your page. Facebook check-in deals allow you to offer special incentives when people check in with your page.

Keep it short and sweet. Want to capture the most eyeballs? Then keep your posts to 80 characters or less. Longer posts tend to be skimmed over and shorter ones tend to get read. You also want to Pin your posts. No, we're not talking about Pinterest here. Rather, Facebook allows you to "pin" a post to the top of your timeline for as long as a week. Use this to showcase something important, such as an upcoming event or a dynamite testimonial from a celeb in your niche.

Grow Your Facebook Page

Make sure to pay special attention to your about section. If you have not touched it since you first created your page, you may need to spruce it up. Let your visitors know what differentiates your business and problems you can solve for them. This section should also include your tagline, call to action and a link that links to your website.

Consider getting some Facebook ads. One of the easiest ways to increase your Facebook likes is through the use of Facebook Ads, which allow you to target specific demographics, which means it will allow you to bring the traffic you desire to your page. It's easy, you can spend as little as you like, and you can target your campaigns to only those people who are likely to be interested in what you have to offer. A Facebook Ad shows up when a person is browsing their News Feed, so they likely don't have any intent to purchase from you at that time. That means you must offer incentives to drive clicks on the Facebook Ad using one of the three methods – coupons, contests, or eBooks. These Facebooks ads let you target those who haven't already likes your page. You can even include a like button right on your ad. You can use the basic format '"Like" us to (insert what they'll receive)'. You can drive Likes based on the incentive. Here are a few you can use:

* Like us and get your Free Guide to Growing Your Facebook Business

* Like us to get an Exclusive 20% Off coupon

* Like us to win a $200 Marketing Consultation

Your goal with your Facebook Page is to grow your Likes and your fan base. To do that you need to take advantage of the many tools that can help you to create a powerful Facebook Ad. Facebook ads are still one of the most misunderstood opportunities to grow your Facebook Page and increase your targeted traffic and your likes. The rest is up to you. With the use of strong posts that engage your followers you can increase your reach further and continue to grow your Page. Everyone likes a discount so maybe once every couple of months offer your followers an exclusive coupon or discount.

Take Advantage of Public Events, they are often overlooked, yet a powerful tool that can be a great way to spread the word. If you are doing public speaking be sure you include your Facebook Page URL on the slide show as it makes it easy for people to connect. If you attend network meetings this is a great time to encourage members to 'Like' your Facebook Page and become fans.

Encourage Check Ins! For anyone who has a brick and mortar business, you should enable check ins on your business page, and then remind customers to check in when they are in your premises. You can even include an incentive like offering a discount. You also want to make sure you are making Use of Signage. When customers visit your brick and mortar business, you can create signs for your store that allows customers to 'Like" your page using a text message. Your sign would look something like this. "Text Like (insert Facebook Page name) to 34587. Test this on your cell phone first to make sure everything is working properly. You can also develop signs that includes your social media icons.

Host a Facebook contest. Run your contest in conjunction with an event or holiday and choose prizes that appeal to your audience such as a free product that you carry or a gift card. You could increase your followers by running a referral contest. A referral contest is when your followers are asked to refer someone or tag their friends in your post and every person that they refer adds to their chances of winning. Photo contest has proven time and time again to be very successful. You can have your followers submit a photo and every person who votes on their photo adds to their chance of winning. At the end of the contest whomever has the most votes win the contest. For the nonwinners you can create a follow-up post offering a discount for the prize that they entered to win. How do you Get People Who Want to Enter Your Contest to Like Your Page and Become a Fan? There are several 3rd party contest apps that you can choose from, such as Wishpond that have a very useful feature, which is called Like Gate, designed to hide the contest entry page until after Liking the Facebook Page. Like Gate is an image that has text that tells the visitor that they must Like the page before they can access the amazing contest. Once they Like it the app automatically loads the default entry for the contest or the voting page where the user enters your contest.

Go Live! This is the best way for your followers to get to know you and your personality. Your live should be valuable to your audience and give them some information or a topic that they are highly interested in, that way they will want to share your content and invite their friends to watch as well. It will help viewing if you announce ahead of time when you will be going live, you can also create an event so that people see when you will be on. Make sure that you have an outline and some main talking points so that you will not just be rambling, and you look more put together and polished. And always make sure to include a call to action during your live, such as to join your FB group, sign up for your e-course, win something or simply to share your live.

It all comes back to providing good content. What is Good Content? Good content will play on life, living situations and interests of your target market. It can be related to day-to-day life and should provoke a personal response immediately. It relates to all kinds of content, asks for the opinion of users, and tells interesting stories. What it does is create a town square attitude where users gather to socialize and find something interesting to engage with likeminded people. Good content is great, but great content is greater. It is very important to have content that is shareable. This means your content is so good that your audience doesn't just want to like it, they want to share it with their own friends. The content that your fans share is really part of their online identity. It tells others what they like and who they are. In this case it also shows support for you. When content is shareable, it increases your likes because it exposes your name to more people, putting your brand out there in front of those that are not currently your fans. If you are unsure of how to create strong content, then have a look at some of the Facebook pages created and managed by large companies such as Proctor & Gamble.

You can create this kind of content by defining your target market and then determining what relevant topics are for that market. You should have a brand strategy and voice that you should stick to so that people what to expect when they visit your page. You may also want to change your cover photo regularly or for holidays and special events so that your page doesn't become stale and boring. Then create themed content that you can schedule so that you have constant posts going out to your users. Facebook group and fan pages now have the option for you to schedule your post out at a later date. If you are anything like me and have a million task in my planner on a daily basis then using this feature is a must and helps keep my business page looking loved. Your goal is to continue to grow your fans through 'Likes' and for them to love what you offer so much that they tell their friends who in turn tell their friends and that reach can continue to expand and grow, offering you a very powerful marketing opportunity.

Best Kept Secrets to Growing Your Facebook Fans

1. Develop a persona for your audience. Some businesses have a description of what their ideal customer looks like. This can help you to visualize your communication and what your posts should look like on Facebook.

2. Install an Engagement App on your Facebook Page. There are many great apps on the market that can help you to accomplish this such as Booshaka or Fan of the Week.

3. If you have several page admins, take advantage of the latest page admin settings that lets you assign authority to each person. Go to your Admin Panel then 'Edit Page' where from the drop-down menu you select 'Admin Roles'. Once on the page you will see the Profile Pic of each Admin with their current role. To change their current role, just click on the down arrow to the right of the current role title and make your selection.

4. Sort your post insights so that at a glance you can see your most successful updates. Go into your insights. On the first page you'll see real time post specific statistics, click on the arrow at the top to sort the updates based on which have gotten the most engagements.

5. If you are using Pinterest, why not install the Pinterest app on your Facebook page.

6. Add the 'Message Button' to your Facebook Page so readers can send you a private message. This also lets you reply privately.

7. Take advantage of Insights to learn more about your fans, their age, sex, where they are from, etc. This will help you with your marketing.

8. Boost The Posts That Are Important Use 'Boosted Posts' to help you increase your audience reach. Enter the amount you are going to set aside for your promotion and Facebook immediately tells you how many people that reach will generate. You can target your reach so that your message is getting to the right people. For example, you can create posts that reach people near you. This

is a powerful tool that is often overlooked because users don't understand its full benefit. It's cost effective and it provides an easy way to expand the reach of your posts. It's important to realize that just posting your post isn't enough anymore. You need to take these extra steps to get the most from your posts.

9. Give Your Page a Facelift It's time to do a little remodeling on your page and add some value. Make sure that your content information and hours of operation are posted. Update your cover photo so that it is current and relevant. Tell your audience a little bit about yourself and your business.

10. Don't Promote, Share – Your Facebook Page doesn't exist just to market your products/services. If that's all you do with it, your followers will lose interest quickly. Use your Page to get people interested that would make use of your products/services.

11. Make Sure You Are Relevant – Think about your posts, keeping in mind the season, what topics are hot, what's in the news, etc. Share links that your fans would be interested in and that they would want to share with their friends.

12. Make Sure Your Posts Are Interesting – Posts don't have to be news to be interesting. Your fans aren't going to be interested in news unless it's relevant, but they might be interested in learning about a new product that's coming to the market that's relevant. For example, let's say that you run a medical page, and there's a new cancer treatment that has shown promising results. Sharing this information with your fans would be wise as it is interesting, engaging, and relevant.

13. Keep Your Fans Talking – Never underestimate the power of your words. 'What's your opinion?' When you post links from experts, especially 'hot topics' or controversial topics, ask your audience for their opinion, their feedback. Your goal is to generate conversation with your fans and to bring new fans on board.

Tips to Increase Your Facebook Likes

1. If you have created a personal profile page for your business instead of a business page this is against Facebook's Terms and Conditions, so you will want to migrate your profile to a new business page. Migrating allows you to do this without losing all your connections. The Facebook migration tool is found at https://www.facebook.com/help?page=213602951994043

2. Create a shorter customized URL for your page. A shorter URL is easy for your visitors to remember and it is easily promoted. Add your Facebook URL to all of your marketing opportunities such as letterhead, business cards, brochures, etc.

3. Caption your photos with your marketing message. Add a caption to all of your images/photos to provide people with more information about your business. Include a call-to-action, a hyperlink, etc.

4.Take the time to create a calendar for your Facebook Page. Planning is very important and planning what you are going to post about in advance and then scheduling it in your editorial calendar can be very helpful. Planning in advance what you want to post about helps you to schedule and organize your themes. This creates an environment where you can tie themes together with what's going on in the community, online, etc. and then you can create valuable material that gains even more power because of your 'timing.'

5. Increase Facebook Likes Using Ebooks. Depending on your industry, education can be a better incentive than even offering a prize or a discount. This is especially true with B2B companies who like to receive free e-books with information and tools to help them grow their business. This is a great way to drive large numbers of visitors to your page and increase your fans significantly. You are dealing with a targeted audience, which is exactly what you want. If you aren't sure what your eBooks should be about consider what your business is about and what you can share with your potential customers that will be useful and hook them on what you have to offer. Your eBook should also include a strong call to action that has the

reader wanting to know more and wanting to take advantage of the service(s) you offer.

6. Invite a couple of others on board as Admin of your Page. They can then suggest it to their friends and your reach can grow. In addition, having more than one administrator can offer different perspectives, which can help to keep the page interesting. It can also make responding to posts and comments more efficient. As your page grows, the more admins you should consider having.

7. If you have a large email list, you can suggest to those on your list to 'Like' your Facebook Page. You might also tell your Twitter followers to come over and 'Like' your page.

These simple tips can help you to grow your Facebook Page. Get ready to enjoy more likes and fans to build your business and increase your sales.

Things You Should Add to Your Facebook Fan Page

Facebook continues to be one of the most popular social media sites growing at thousands of users a day. Because of the vast background of all these users it doesn't take a lot of effort to recognize its influence, and any company, regardless of size and product will be able to boost their brand and create product familiarity, while always building potential customers. It's easy to create a Facebook page, but what many are not aware of is that creating a Facebook page that easily collects 'likes' and builds a strong fan base, is a daunting task.

When a visitor makes it to your Facebook page, most will click on either your info or wall, and if they don't find anything that catches their interest, they will simply leave your page. When a visitor likes your page, it's to your advantage, because this new fan will be updated now and then with things you publish. You may have come across pages on Facebook that are so well done you wonder how it was possible. Great news! Here are 7 things you need to know about your Facebook fan page.

#1 Product Commenting! If you want to set up a little store on your Facebook business page, this feature is excellent. You have each product liked and then commented on.

#2 Insert Flash Content! If you want to customize your Facebook fan pages with flash files for the header or in the photo gallery you will need to install a plugin or widget like 3D Flash Slide Show Maker. There are others that you can research and use as well.

#3 Use Social Plug Ins and Website Widgets Install social plug ins like Facebook Like Box or Wibiya Toolbar on your website or blog, which allow your visitors to 'Like' your Facebook page right from your website. There are many other plug ins that you can install easily to the back end of your website.

#4 Email Signatures An often-overlooked way to grow your Facebook Page fans is to include an email signature on all your emails. It's easy to implement and very effective. If you are like most businesses, every day you send out a number of emails and so having the link to your social networking sites on your emails promotes your growth.

#5 Featured Likes You can display as many as 5 'Featured Likes.' These are Pages that are liked by your Page on your Facebook Page. Another excellent technique to use is to ask your Featured Likes to return the favor for you. This gives you a little advertising boost.

#6 Create a Newsletter If you haven't already taken the step to create a newsletter to send out to your customers and fans, then now is the perfect time to do just that. MailChimp along with other providers provide a simple newsletter solution. You can also post on your Facebook Page when your newsletter is available. Do a good job and provide valuable content so that your fans share it and you grow your fan base.

#7 Comment on the Business Pages of Others! If you want to get more Facebook fans, then you need your page to be as visible as you can possibly make it to a relevant audience. If you are a local brick and mortar business, you should 'Like' other local pages. Make comments on their pages as your page not your personal name. If you comment on posts where others have already commented, depending on their settings, they will be notified that you posted giving you increased visibility.

How To Use Facebook Live To Connect With Your Audience

Word travels very fast on Facebook. If the right people get a hold of your idea and run with it, you can get massive free exposure that can lead to equally impressive sales. So why not step things up a bit with your own live Facebook event. It's easy to start your own chat session or webinar. You can use a simple, free software called Linq to (pronounced Link-to) to easily host your teleseminar on your

Facebook account. Use a mic and webcam to connect with others who can do the same. These days most recent laptops, desktops, and pads have mics and cams built in, so it's a no-brainer to host this kind of live event.

What can you talk about in your Facebook webinar?

1) Show people how to do something. Teach what you know. Keep it basic or focus entirely on one complex aspect many people have difficulty with.

2) Announce your new product or service and demonstrate how it works. Ask for comments and ideas on how the product can be used. Or ask for ideas on how an old product can be improved.

3) Hold a meeting of your "trusted advisors." Your customers can give you input on what moves your company should make. People love to voice their ideas and opinions.

4) Announce and explain a new business opportunity. In the new economy, there will be many hidden chances to earn good incomes in ways we may not have noticed before.

Live events have always gotten attention on the Web. From the very beginning live chats with experts, live webcams, and later live events on YouTube got lots of interest and even made headlines. That principle hasn't changed. The Internet is largely static, with pages of writing that change little from day to day or even year to year. One of the things that people like most about Facebook is it's always changing. There are always fresh posts and photos being added moment to moment.

You can take this idea one step further by hosting a live event. As one expert put it, get the right event on Facebook and it's like throwing gasoline on a fire. Staging your own live event on Facebook is putting an exciting twist on the world's most popular gathering place. You may be surprised at the audience and fans you draw in.

Bring Your A-Game

The Thunderpenny app allows you to add your own pre-created landing page. You can add this static html app to your page and link it to an existing landing page. Here are the steps:

- Add the tab to your business page
- Choose the 'website' option
- Copy the URL from your landing page to the website
- Click 'remove scroll bars' to manually adjust the size of the landing page within Facebook
- Click 'save and publish'
- Use Canva to create a custom graphic for the tab (dimensions 111 x 74)
- Add the image to the tab – navigate to the 'welcome tab' and hover over it. This will bring up an 'edit setting' option.
- Change the tab name to the call-to-action that you choose and upload the newly created image

All Done!

Would you like your followers to be able to schedule a one on one session with you or to share their thoughts or feedback about your products or services? If so then you should add a contact form to your page. Here's how:

Go to https://www.facebook.com/contact.form, click Use Now, select which page you would like to add it to and click okay. Easy, peasy!

Videos are a great way to increase engagement and boost your sales. Statics show that 64% of consumers are more likely to make a purchase after watching a video. You could create a behind the scenes video or if you want to show off your product, make a video of the product arriving, and create a funny scenes sequence. You could also create a short video of a customer receiving your product and their reaction when it arrives. Act and write script for your video like you would speak in real life. That is the key to connect with your audience. Planned streams are a great way to build anticipation with your audience. By letting them know ahead of time, creating a flyer, tweeting and including in your newsletter when you will broadcast will give them something to look forward to. On the day that you go live make sure to add a tempting description, you can also add hashtags and tag friends as well. When you are done your live video will be published and saved to your wall, you will also have the option to save the video to your device which is handy if you would like to upload the content to YouTube for more exposure.

If you have a blog, follow these simple steps to get the most out of your video content. First you want to upload your video to YouTube, create a short blog post explaining what your video is about, add bullet points highlighting the content of your video, grab the direct link to your video from YouTube and add it to your blog post as a hyperlink, you then want to share your blog post to your Facebook business page. A few days later share the video minus the blog post with a short description and a call to action.

7 WAYS YOU CAN MAKE MONEY ON FACEBOOK

1. **Drive traffic to your website and build your mailing list**
2. **Affiliate Marketing**
3. **Facebook Events**
4. **Offering Facebook and social media management services**
5. **Networking for joint ventures**
6. **Create groups around your niche and promote your products or services**
7. **Promote Clickbank offers**

FACEBOOK QUICK TIPS

1. Invite your Facebook friends from your personal profile to like your business page.
2. Post interesting, relevant, useful updates two to four times a day to benefit from viral growth.
3. Have a link to your fan page on every page of your website and in the signature section of your emails.
4. Offer a great incentive for people to become a fan.
5. Go to Fiverr.com and pay people $5 to promote your Facebook page to all of their friends or twitter followers.
6. Hire outsourcers to invite relevant Facebook users to become fans of your page. Sites where you can find outsources are Elance.com, Freelancer.com, Guru.com, ContentDivas.com, 123Emplyoee.com, Scriptlance.com, Hiremymom.com and Peopleperhour.com
7. Link with other Facebook entrepreneurs and suggest doing a free of charge cross promotion.
8. Use Facebook Ads to pay for traffic to your Fan page.

Google +

Google+ is still the new kid on the social media block and was created to compete with Facebook and Twitter. With more than 500 million users who share more than 1 billion pieces of content every day, most users are still treating it like the red headed step child, this may be due to a slow adoption and a tricky interface. However, Google+ hopes to have more social connections and key features than any other applications and programs to date.

Google is everywhere. From Google Search engine to Google maps, Google Earth to Google Docs, Gmail, GChat, GCal, Google Play to Google Chrome Web Browser. And surprisingly people still think that Google + is a ghost town. That is actually the best reason to get active on the app because as long as your competitors keep believing that it is not beneficial, you have an advantage to dominate the market. It is true that Google plus is still small compared to other social sites like Facebook and Instagram. With such large platforms that means that it is harder to build a large audience there. Goggle+ users tend to be more thoughtful and highly engaged people. With that being said they are worth finding and a small number of Google+ followers can bring you more value than a larger audience on other networks. With increased engagement on Google + it can provide your business with lots of exposure when approached correctly.

A lot of business owners write off Google plus because they don't understand search engine marketing. Search engine marketing looks way beyond your number of likes and followers to strategies that maximize reach and influence. That is because of Google+'s tight integration into Google search. Your post on Google plus are easily indexed by google search and unlike other social media posts, are treated more like regular web pages. That means a well-constructed G+ post with a main keyword in the first sentence or title & a good amount of engagement can rank high on google search and stay ranked for a long time. I have a few G+ posts that have built around keywords that are important to me that have been in the top 3 on google search for up to 12 months. Let's not forget Googles personalized search. Analytics show that for business sites 70% or more of your users are logged into Google while using the web and their results are highly personalized. Via google plus, google will rank those sites endorsed by others in a persons extended network. So, the bigger your google+ network, the bigger the range of people whose search results will show you higher in rank. Thanks to my network on Google plus, I am now getting offers to speaking events, request to write for well known blogs, and even gotten clients to sign up for my book publishing coaching sessions. In this section on the book my hopes are to help you optimize your Google plus account, build traffic, increase engagement and discover new people and content on the G+ platform. As with all social media platforms your SEO does not depend on how many people follow you, it is about your engagement, relevance and authority that counts. Keep reading to get some tips to help you get more from your Google Plus profile and how to use the Google + features.

The Google+ social network has a collection of products intended to interest every user. You'll want to explore its newsfeed called Stream, a video chat service known as Hangouts, Sparks a recommendation engine, Circles which is a friend management service (how you organize the people you connect with), Photos to share with your favorite people, and Huddle which is a texting service for groups of people. Since Google considers Google+ as an extension of itself, you'll notice in the Google navigation bar that it now includes a link to your Google+ profile. With all the other visual changes that Google has associated with

Google+, you will now be able to see the number of notifications you've received. This is similar to the way Facebook would let you know how many notifications you have once you're logged into your account.

The purpose of Google + is to connect all of your Google activity and link them back to you and your brand. Four reasons why you should create a Google + business page is for increased brand discovery, more engagement, better marketing performance across the web and to have the ability to measure your impact. When creating your business page make sure that you select the correct category and include your website URL. Add an interesting tagline. This is super important for your hover card. Your tagline will show up on your profile underneath your name. When go to your page they will get a feel for what you are about, and this will determine whether to add you. Create a simple yet significant tagline that will easily catch people's attention. You don't have to be a copywriter to create a great tagline. In fact, a short, simple, straightforward, and even an emotional tagline will do just fine.

Your About Page is the influential part of your Google+ profile. It is basically your online resume. A well thought out About page will help you achieve higher rankings in Google search also completing the Introduction and Contributor section will assist in helping you claim authorship of your blog, blog posts and articles that you have written online. To establish authorship simply add your blog or website to the contributor section, then on the home tag select the user profile that matches to your google plus profile. The lengthier and keyword rich your introduction is the easier it will be for people to find you. This would be the section where you get to introduce yourself and be more personal. People add you because they want to learn more about you, so its important to share who you are and what you are about. Make this section a bit more interesting by adding your personal story, hobbies, favorite quotes, etc. You may also want to add your mission statement, what your business does and some interesting facts about your brand.

Also let your audience know that you are present on other social media sites. You may want to include your contact information such as your business address, phone number and email address. When selecting your profile picture, keep in mind that your image appears circular while in the app but in the google search results it will show up a square. This may create an issue when using a logo. You may have to make your logo smaller or use a different image all together. When uploading your cover photo make sure to fully optimize it by incorporating keywords into your cover photos filename and add a relevant description to the caption. When you are done setting up your page make sure that verify your email address. A profile with a verified email is more appealing and looks more authentic and professional than non-verified ones. Once you verify your email you will notice a little checkmark icon beside your email address.

Fill out all of the fields that are available. Add your skills, work history, where you live (city & state) and your education information. For maximum optimization make yourself sound as impressive as possible so that you have an attention-grabbing hover card that will be a solid first impression, thus gaining you more targeted followers.

The fastest and easiest way to add a Google+1 button to your website, is to access this URL and follow the instructions:
http://www.google.com/webmasters/+1/button/index.html

The +1 button icons are available in four heights: small (15px), medium (20px), standard (24px), and tall (65px). Several button sizes, including the tall button will allow the counts that indicate the number of times someone has +1'd an item on your site.

Tag Someone in a Post.

Facebook uses the "@" symbol followed by someone's name to tag a person in a stats update. To tag a person in an update on Google+, type the +symbol, followed by their username. As you type, Google+ will autofill possible options. When you tag someone, they get a notification which is a good way to attract attention and kick off some conversation.

Circles are how you organize the people that you connect with. The best way to do this is to group them by your work relation, interest, hobbies, humor, travel and activities. You can also have one person in more than one circle if you want. After you create your circles you can chose to show content from one circle on your feed at a time or which circle that you want to share your post to. To share a circle that you are in on your profile go to your home page, click the menu n the top left corner and select people. Click your circles and at the bottom of the screen select the circle that you want to share, click actions and then choice share this circle.

You can also send a private message to someone by using the share box. Simply change the public option to the specific person that you want to send the message to, write your message and share. To get more activity on your post tag certain people or you can include an entire circle by adding them in the "to" box at the top of your post.

Tips for building your following

- Be yourself and post content that is interesting to you and that resonates with your audience.
- Make sure your cover photo is pleasing to the eye and on theme with your brand.
- Add your other social media links to your G+ profile and add the G+ button to your blog post if you have a blog.
- Make sure your profile is up to date and matches your brands overall theme.
- Interact with people, share their content and comment on their posts.
- Sharing images, infographics, and videos more than text post.
- Post frequently, once or twice a day is ideal.
- Search for other users with similar interests, you can use # to find people or check out the circles of other people you follow.
- Watch for people sharing circles, this is a great way to find lots of great people to follow quickly and easily.
- Add your business as your employer by editing your setting.
- Connect your YouTube account
- Add descriptions to your content
- Use Call to actions such as questions, asking for shares and +1s
- Use relevant hashtags
- Treat your Google+ like your mini blog
- Add your Google+ page to your email signature

Make sure you are updating your Google Plus page on a regular basis. The content needs to be exclusive, valuable, and compelling, both in terms of visuals and substance. Knowing that Google Plus posts are searchable, you should treat them like Micro Blog (and a very powerful one at that). For your business page, you should keep the content strictly on topic, but periodically post content on other areas of interest.

Watch for Trending Topics to Find Out What Your Users Are Talking About. Use the explore feature to check out what's hot in your niche. Keep tabs on trending topics, and it will give you an idea as to what kinds of posts, images, or GIFs are getting exposure among your target audience. In most cases, you will notice that a lot of content is not very creative, or entirely original. Again, your content needs to be on topic in case of a business page (though you can use polls, questions, or surveys to make it more engaging). Figure the Optimal Time to Post for Your Audience. Rotate post time until you figure out when you get the best results. Depending on the age group, time zone, or occupation of your target market, posts or updates made at different times can yield significantly different results. Not that the quality of your post doesn't matter but knowing the optimal time to post is important for getting maximum exposure and response from your target audience. And, the only way to figure that out is to test and compare. If it's not feasible to post manually at a specific time on a regular basis, you can use a tool like Buffer for custom scheduling.

Hangouts On Air are a great way to brand yourself or your business as an expert. If you are an authority on your subject (or you can get an expert on board), Google hangouts-on-air can be a great platform to engage and impress you target users. While it will take quite some time to plan, prepare, and promote a hangout on air, it's worth the effort. You can build a good following by organizing a successful hangout every once in a while, and it can be a nice step toward establishing yourself as an authority. Google Hangouts helps your brand engage on a more personal level. You can video chat with people all over the world, host virtual meetings, stream and record conversations for playback later or broadcast live events such as concerts, shows or conferences. I have personal hosted live interviews, showed some behind the scenes footage and showed sneak peaks of my Fall collection to drive traffic to my webpage. You can use Hangouts to develop your reputation as an industry influencer by sharing your opinions, connection with others in your field, staying on top of the latest news and teaching your audience something by offering tips on a subject that you are very knowledgeable in. You could consider hosting a weekly Hangout to give your audience something to look forward to. Create Events and Invite Your Followers. Be social and create events through Google+. To promote your hangout, create a circle of Google Plus users that you are looking to target. Create an Event for your hangout and send the invitation to the people in that particular circle. Use a compelling title and banner to entice more people. Also encourage the invitees to share the news with their contacts. And make it a public event so that anybody can participate (unless you'd like some sort of restriction on attendees).

In the Google plus communities like minded people come together to have conversations and to discuss content over shared interest such as food, fashion, art, music. Etc. Google communities are equivalent to Facebook groups. This is a great way for brands to listen to what the consumer has to say. You should be participating in communities within your industry and sharing interesting and valuable content. You join communities because they are helpful to you, you get benefits. Or you can start your own Private or Public community. Share some helpful information as well and the return will be hundredfold. Be friendly, talk to the people, respond and make meaningful comments on the community post. People want to see you in human form that actually communicates and are interested in people. Once you have made some friends follow the active people that interest you, most likely they will follow you back. Connecting with the influential members of google+ can do wonders for your account growth. If a person that is influential in topics relevant to yours engage with your content, it will have a bigger impact on your rating. There are many ways to do this, mention them in your post, comment on their content, add them to your circles, or directly share a post with them. Another way that I grow my followers easily is by going to a popular post and following those people who shared or commented on the post. I do this because I know that they are active and may share my content as well. To find Influencers go to your home screen, click on Explore from the top menu and then click What's Hot. From there you will be able to see the most shared and liked posts.

Sharing circles and getting included in other peoples shared circles is virtually expanding your horizon and widening your opportunities for a higher reputation. It also makes your profile more visible. However, if you want targeted followers be careful of which circles you add. You can build a circle of people around a certain topic and then share that circle in a post. Other people can add the circle to their own circles with one click. Mention the influential that you included in your circle and they are almost certain to reshare it with own network. By taking these steps you can singlehandedly leverage Google+ for your personal branding to become an established leader in your Niche. We have talked about setting up your profile and how to gain new followers, now let's take a look at why it makes sense for all professionals to have a google plus presence, and how in doing so it can help you develop a robust personal brand.

Make sure you are utilizing your links sections by connecting your other social media profiles. Google will automatically find your other profiles on the web, you simply select the ones that you want included. Websites and blogs with Google authorship rank higher in search results and your post on Google plus get indexed faster in google search results giving added credibility and authority. Place your Google Plus profile in the author bio whenever you get a chance to be featured as a guest author on other blogs. Not only will you get some followers (if the guest post and the blog are good enough), it also will contribute to your author rank. Your profile is treated like a webpage by google which is why your links get up to 30%-150% increased visibility.

Content is king so sharing great content is required to excite your google plus friends and to attract more followers. You should be sharing interesting content consistently. This could be infographics, videos, questions, a free eBook offer, and funny photos. Do you know why newspapers and magazines are so popular? Because one issue is not the same as the last. You want to work your page the same way by always giving something new to your audience. And Don't be afraid to ask people to +1 and share your post. When someone +1 your posts, it will appear in the feed of people who are following them. And there's nothing wrong with asking people to +1 your post if they like it (needless to say, you need to make it like-worthy first). For some, it might sound a little desperate, but, at times, a simple call to action can make the difference. Also Use your real-world contacts to build up your numbers initially. Don't forget to invite your friends, colleagues, customers, and any other contacts to like or follow your business page. It's good to have some followers (especially for small businesses) because, just like money begets money, page likes, or followers beget more page likes and followers.

Optimize your post for more engagement. Doesn't it feel good when you get a lot of likes, shares and comments? When you create a post do not just share a link or picture, make sure to include a description of what your content is about and always use high quality images and relevant hashtags. Just like on other social sites hashtags help people search for related content or follow threads bases on a particular hashtag. G+ suggests hashtags as you type which helps you to use ones that are most popular at the moment. You may also notice that hashtags will automatically be assigned for you on your content if you do not add them. Adding a call to action such as a link to your blog or other social media site is a win all the way around. You also want to be mindful that you are sharing other people's content. Sharing someone else's work makes you look interested in them and in return they will come check out your profile. If you don't have time to create a post or share new content daily, try using an auto scheduling tool.

TWITTER FOR BUSINESS

There's no doubting it. You can barely turn on the TV, look in a newspaper or log onto the internet these days without seeing something about Twitter. In this section, we are going to talk a little bit about what Twitter is and how you can take advantage of everything it has to offer. One of the things that makes Twitter so popular is that it's extremely easy to use even though it is a very powerful platform. With Twitter, you can follow other users, make connections and tweet updates, which makes it a fun and interactive form of communication. Twitter is used by all kinds of people – from private individuals who use it to keep track of their interests and follow people they know, through to celebrities who use it to promote themselves and communicate with fans, and businesses of all sizes – from small local firms through to global multinational organizations.

When it comes to marketing any type of business, product or service online it is always good to have a social media presence and Twitter makes that very easy. It gives you the opportunity to interact with your consumers on a more personal level. When you think about it, it doesn't really take a genius to figure out why Twitter is good for businesses... Any tool which gives us the ability to communicate with customers is extremely powerful – and what makes something like Twitter even more so is that it encourages conversations between companies and customers. These conversations are an excellent way of building relationships with customers and can help you to make more money and engage better with your clients. So – Twitter is great for business and it's great for us as internet marketers. Through Tweets you can post links to your products and websites, keep people up to date with 'what you're up to' (for example if you're working on a new product) and it also allows people to see that you are human – which is very important!

In case you aren't familiar with Twitter it's a cross between a micro-blog and a social networking site. It's free to use, which makes it an excellent tool for advertising. Once you become a member, you can share updates with other members. These short updates are called tweets, which are limited to 140 characters or less. Depending on your personal preferences, updates can be sent via multiple devices like your PC, Mac or mobile devices like laptops, tablets and phones. There are also array applications that you can use to manage your account like Hootsuite, InTweets and SnapBird. If you're a Mac user, you can use the Twitterrific desktop program. It allows you to send from your computer without first logging into Twitter.

For the most part, Twitter is used for social networking. Members can message their friends with fun and interesting updates on any given topic. Although popular with teens and adults of all ages, Twitter is very popular with college students. It allows them to stay in contact with their family and friends back home. As a business owner, there are many ways you can use Twitter to your advantage. Whether you operate a large business or a small one, it can give your business an edge over the competition. Although most users frown upon blatant advertising, there are roundabout ways for you to market your business, which we will discuss later on in the chapter. Whether you're selling a product, service, or a combination of the two, you can use Twitter to spread the word about what you have to offer. For example, if you're a web designer you can post tweets to your followers about you latest projects and designs. In the event a follower needs a website developed, they will most likely remember your messages and the services you offer first because you've developed a rapport with them.

As you can see, Twitter is more than just a social networking site. If you aren't already one of the 200 million users who have tried it, now is the time. All you have to do is go sign up and start tweeting. Since it's free, you have nothing to lose and a lot of free exposure to gain. Are you already using Twitter? If you are than chances are, you're only using it to communicate with a few followers, friends and family. As we discussed earlier, this is the most common use of this massive social network; however, it has the potential to be so much more. When properly managed, it can be a very effective marketing tool.

Simply hearing that Twitter is a great marketing tool is nice, but like many business owners and entrepreneurs, you may be a little lost and confused when it comes to understanding why. That's why we are going to discuss some of the best reasons why you should start using it to market your business, products and services right away. Your online presence is an extension of the brand you have built offline. In order to translate that you need to focus on the look, feel and intention of your brand.

Ask yourself a few questions:

- How does my brand make people feel and how will that be seen, heard and felt online?
- What is the purpose and what is the brand you are trying to build?
- How will my content extend the mission and vision of my brand?

You need to be clear about the brand message you are trying to convey. This is a vital factor to keep in mind if you want to use Twitter to build your personal brand.

Reach a large market

As we already know, there are well over 200 million active users on Twitter and it is rapidly growing in popularity every day. When it comes to marketing, this gives you almost instant access to a large audience of consumers who are interested in what you have to offer. While you won't be able to communicate will all the members, the potential of reaching a targeted percentage of them is very powerful. The first place to start is by making connections and building a list of followers. One place to start is to search Twitter for other users who are interested in the types of products and services you offer. You can also search for members based on email address, name, and location. Of course, you can add anyone to your list of contacts, but it's more effective to aim for your targeted market. You can even indicate that you only want tweets from specific accounts or from those mentioning certain accounts. Now it's time to jump into the conversation and begin a dialogue with those tweeting and talking about subjects surrounding your industry or niche. Once you have completed that task, add these industry leaders to a Twitter list. Similar to Facebook lists, Twitter allows you to categorize those people you follow into targeted lists. If you are lazy (nothing wrong with that) you can even use other peoples list, subscribe to them and save yourself the time to create your own list. This will allow you to come in on a daily basis and quickly and easily keep up with those you want to begin to build relationships with. Your next step is to visit your list and start replying to tweets, sharing one of their tweets with your audience or visiting their blog and commenting on their latest post. If you are new to Twitter, you may not realize that you can create your personal or business brand and virtually dominate your market, simply by setting up a profile and building a list of followers.

Once you've set up your Twitter account you'll want to work on your profile. Take time to customize the look and feel of your page so that it reflects the products and services you offer. Pay close attention to your bio, because this is what people will read before they decide whether they want to follow you. You only have 160 characters to describe who you are and what you do, so you have to make it good! You'll also want to add a good profile picture and header photo to make your business attractive and memorable. Next, you'll want to start growing your list of followers. If you already have a list of business contacts, you can jumpstart the process by inviting them to follow you. Start by putting link's in your emails, on your websites and blogs asking people to follow you. You can take it a step further by putting your Twitter URL on your business card, so that you can gather followers offline as well.

So – how do you get followers?

Well we'll get onto that in a moment but first I want to define between two types of followers:

The first type of followers are people who are following you because you are following them. Many reports teach you to follow lots of people in the hope that they will follow you back. This is an excellent strategy but only in the short term. It's a great way to get started (I'll show you how to do it below) but over the long term what you really want are the second type of followers – people who follow you because they want to follow you! I hope you can see the difference between the two there. The first type may be operating in your niche market, but they may not be directly interested in your tweets. What you really need are people who actively read your tweets and click on your links – and those people usually fall into the second category.

First of all, make a list of anyone you know of who is big in your niche. Your job now is to find them on Twitter. Once you are on their profile look at who is following THEM, and then follow them. Why would we want to do this? Well if you think about it, the fact that they are following one of our competitors shows that they must have some sort of interest in the niche. If someone is following Mike Filsaime then you can be pretty sure they are interested in internet marketing! If someone is following Alan Titchmarsh (a well-known gardener in the UK) then you can be pretty sure they are interested in gardening! By following these people, you will find that a certain percentage of them follow you back. Your job now, then, is to follow 200 or 300 people using the method I have just outlined above. Do this over a couple of days and you will find that fairly quickly you start to generate some followers. Continue doing this until you get your first 100 followers, then your next 100 followers. Tracking and measuring your online results are an important part of your strategy. Staying on top of what is working and what is not is a proactive way to observe how your content, message, voice and overall personal brand is received. Topsy, which provided detailed Twitter search results, recently rolled out Twitter analytics. While this information was available on certain tweets, the ability to see trends and sentiment on all tweets is a welcome change. Use Topsy to measure your own day-to-day or compare yourself to two additional competitors.

Have you ever saw a tweet in your feed that you find interesting but do not have time to explore further at the present moment? How will you ever find this tweet later? Heart it! When you heart a tweet, you can then go to your profile later and go to the heart tab. All tweets that you hearted are there, ready for you to read later.

While there are no rules against advertising on Twitter, there are rules against spam. For that reason, avoid sending large, bulky unsolicited advertisements. For example, encourage people to view your latest blog post, but do so no more than twice a day. Any more and your Tweets may be classified as spam. To increase your success, cleverly write your tweets. It's easy to make ads appear as if they aren't even advertisements at all. As I mentioned above all you have to do is briefly discuss your products and ask for feedback. This still gets consumers to view the product, but without the pressure to buy and it will get much more positive results than simply listing products with their selling price. Keep in mind that when you tweet about a product or service that you have to offer, it's an easy way to create a buzz and generate interest. The more interesting you make your product or service sound in your tweets, the more buzz you can generate and the more likely it will be that people comment and share your tweets with others. These are just a few reasons why you should give marketing on Twitter a try. While others use it solely for social purposes, you can easily turn it into an effective promotional tool for your business.

Whether you run a full-fledge online business or if you only sell a few products online, your success depends on marketing. After all, if consumers don't know what you have to offer, you'll never make a profit. For that reason alone, internet marketing is a crucial aspect of your success. The good news is that you have many options, including social media marketing on networks like Twitter. Before focusing on how you can use Twitter to market the products and services you sell, it is important to understand how the system works. As we know, it's an online service that is defined as a social network or micro-blog. If you belong to an online forum or community, create a post asking the other members to check out your Twitter account. Offer to follow them on their accounts. This way they have something to gain by following you and both parties benefit. The goal of your first few messages shouldn't be to sell, but rather to introduce yourself and your business to the network. For instance, your first message could be something like "Still trying to learn my way around the Twitter. Thank you for joining me on the journey." Then, you can work your way into marketing your products. This first personal message gives the impression that you aren't just interested in making contact to sell.

Marketing on any social network is all about being subtle. Instead of saying "Buy a leather office chair from my online store," try something more creative. For example, say, "I just added a new leather office chair to my inventory. Isn't it pretty, what do you think? www.officechairs.com". It's short, to the point and invites your followers to join in the conversation. Yes, you're advertising a product and your message implies so, but you aren't outright asking for a sale, only an opinion. The way you word your tweets can make a huge difference in the response you receive. Twitter members don't want to be bombarded with direct sales offers, but you will find that many like to express their opinions or give feedback. In the end, the results are the same. If someone likes what you're selling, they will buy.

It doesn't matter whether you have a traditional brick and mortar business or sell products and services online, internet marketing is a necessity these days. If you don't have an online presence, you're missing out on the opportunity to connect with potential customers. Think about it, what is the first thing you do when you are thinking about buying something new? For most of us, it's go online and do some research, right? Well, if you don't have an online presence and, in this case, a social media presence chances are, you're missing out on easy sales. Did you know that Twitter profiles and posts (tweets) often show up in the search engine results? It's true, so that means you have the potential to reach a very large and targeted consumer group just by posting useful and relevant tweets.

Before we dive into the rest of this chapter, I want to reinforce the importance of understanding that Twitter, is first and foremost a social networking site and should always be treated as such even when you're using it for marketing. After signing up for an account, it's important to start developing a list of followers and cultivate a relationship with them At first, this will be a list of people that you follow in hopes of reciprocation. Once you start following people many will return the favor, becoming your follower and that's when the magic starts to happen. As your following grows, so will your opportunity to share your marketing messages. Discreetly of course!

Do share the latest news in your niche. This is easy – sign up for Google Alerts using terms relevant to your niche to receive the latest news each day, and then write a few tweets from this content. Presto! That took maybe 5 minutes, and you become the informed person people want to follow. Do offer your Twitter followers sales and coupons. Since the very nature of Twitter is a fast response, you can give followers an incentive to follow you by offering them special deals, such as a 50% discount for the next 20 minutes. Do elicit customer feedback. Ask questions such as, "What's missing from our latest product?" What's your toughest challenge?" "What would you like to know concerning how to _____?" And so forth. This is a great way to get information on how to improve your current products and what products you should roll out next. Be sure to acknowledge the responses you receive. Do run contests. People love contests and you can really capture their interest with this. First, make the contests short –

no more than an hour in duration. Second, make them fun. You might ask followers to send their best example of a web page with a funny header or to guess what you did to earn money in junior high, or to write the best headline for toothpaste for elephants. Encourage your followers to retweet your contest and be sure to award prizes to the winners – free copies of an e-product or Amazon coupons work great. Do run polls. You'll find new people to follow and you'll collect dynamite tips and insights from your followers. Plus, it's a great opportunity to engage your network and further build your relationships. Prepare questions for your audience that will appeal to them. You can use Post Planner to access and schedule from a database of engaging questions. But it's best to speak on the topics that matter to foster value-added conversations.

There are no limits on how many tweets you can post a day. However, there is a 140-character limit, as we well know. But did you know that you can add up to four photos on each tweet and tag up to ten people and still have your 140 characters left for your message? You can also send a direct message (DM) which is a private message sent via Twitter to one of your followers and you can add videos and photos to your DM as well. You can only send DM's to users who are following you and you can only receive them from users you follow. As we have discussed before the key to using Twitter as a marketing tool is to market without directly advertising. You can do this through your tweets and by responding to other people's tweets. Which is a great way to expand your reach and grow your following at the same time. When it comes to finding other people's tweets to comment on you can use the built-in search bar by typing in what you are looking for or typing in a hashtag. From there you can type in keywords and search terms related to the types of products and services you offer. After you type in your query, you will be presented with a list of updates almost like you get when you use Google, Yahoo or Bing. This list will contain various information that you can use to hunt down popular tweets and users to help grow your presence.

When browsing through the list of messages pay close attention to the little icons below the tweet. From there you can tell how many times it has been retweeted (shared), added to favorites and when you click the "more" icon you can do other cool things like send the tweet via DM or email. Look for tweets that are getting a lot of response from other users in terms of retweets and comments. You'll notice the popular tweets come from users who have a lot of followers and post a lot of updates, these are the people you should engage with. Start by following them and responding to their tweets with helpful information. This will get your profile in front of their followers, which will naturally grow your following. Remember, people are curious by nature and you can use that to your advantage by posting interesting information that will make them want to check out what else you have to offer.

As we well know Twitter can be a great marketing tool, but you still may be wondering if marketing your website, blog, products, or service through Twitter is a good idea. In most cases, it is, but as with any new method you try, you should first familiarize yourself with the pros and cons.

- The pros

Twitter is massive and it's free to join, which is a definite plus. All you need is an internet connection. If you don't already have a profile set up, I highly recommend that you go over to Twitter.com and sign up. The process is very easy. All you have to do is select a username, password, and provide your email address. Unlike many other marketing methods, it requires no investment other than time.
Tip: To improve your results, always aim for your target market when you are looking for people to follow.

Your tweets always go to your followers. Unlike other forms of marketing like email, banners ads and even other social sites like Facebook, every tweet goes to all of your followers and posts directly to your Twitter feed for everyone to see. Unless you send a direct message (DM) or tweet directly to someone using the @ symbol, which is used to call out usernames in Tweets.

Ask Siri to tweet for you! Tweet with no hands. If you are not an Apple fan get the social voice app for Android and speak your tweet. How it works: Just say "Send a tweet" and Siri will ask you what you want to tweet. Once your done just confirm with Siri to send. It is not as easy on Android. Social voice works in sync with Google Voice, so it may not be possible to record and send without touching the phone.

Twitter is a high-volume platform. Due to the speed it moves, each tweet has less of a shelf-life than statuses on some other platforms. This means you can afford to share the same content more frequently than you would elsewhere. Each time you tweet something, a big proportion of the people who follow you won't see it, so share your content A lot.

Tweets are easy to create. They take less than a minute to write and send. But, don't let that fool you they can still be very effective when it comes to getting your products and services noticed. Twitter has global reach. You can advertise your website, blog, product or service to people all over the world. In terms of marketing, this gives you a lot of potential. You can use it to build brand recognition, drive traffic, generate interest, as well as increase sales.

- The cons

The biggest con I have found while using Twitter is that it can be addicting and distracting. Yes, your main goal is to use Twitter for marketing, but you may find yourself easily distracted when you start reading other people's messages. The more interesting conversations you join in the more time you may want to spend tweeting.

Many people use it incorrectly and they end up sounding too spammy. If you don't proceed with caution and the majority of your messages sound like advertisements, you won't receive the response you're hoping for. Twitter is about connecting with other users, not solely for soliciting sales online.

Twitter is full of activity. Did you know that users generate over 300 million tweets a day, and most users follow hundreds if not thousands of profiles? This means if you only tweet once or twice a day, your tweets are quickly lost in your follower's feeds.

Twitter isn't great for visual content, while it is evolving to include other forms of media it's still mostly text based. If you want to share a lot of photos, Pinterest or Instagram may be a better idea for hosting them and then sharing them with your Twitter followers in a tweet that includes a link.

And of course, you are limited to 140 characters, which can be a challenge if you have a lot to say. If you have trouble expressing your thoughts in just a few words you can try breaking up your messages into individual sentences that you tweet in a row almost like a story. Just make sure your individual tweets make sense or your followers will get lost in the conversation and loose interest.

Now let's talk about using Twitter to build your email list. Building a list is one of the most important things you can do to help grow your business and market your products and services. What many people don't realize is that Twitter is a great way to get more subscribers. Any time you are marketing on a website that you don't own, you're running the risk that your account could be deleted, or the site could change its terms and terminate your campaign. When you build a list, you will be able to market to that list for many years to come. Best of all, you won't have to worry about breaking Twitter's terms, even if they change the terms later. You can market to your own list any legal way you want!

If you aren't already building an email list the first thing you will need is an autoresponder account in order to manage your list effectively. While there are free autoresponder's available paid accounts with a reputable company is well worth the investment, and you won't have to worry about losing your list of contacts while you are growing your list.

Here are few of the top providers available:
http://www.GetResponse.com
http://www.Aweber.com
http://www.mailchimp.com
http://www.constantcontact.com

All of these services are very good and which one you use will depend on your needs and personal preferences. Once you sign up for your autoresponder account, you will need to add the code to your squeeze page. This form will allow users to enter their name and email address to join your mailing list. A squeeze page is similar to a sales page, but it's shorter and simpler. You need to make sure your squeeze page tells people why they should sign up to your list. You might give away an incentive like a free E-Book, a video tutorial, or a free course that is delivered daily to their email. You can set your autoresponder up to deliver the freebie automatically after they sign up. Just make sure the incentive you offer is relevant to the products and services you are promoting. For instance, if you sell golf clubs you could offer a short report on choosing the right set of clubs or 5 ways you can improve your golf swing over the weekend! Once everything is set up, you can start tweeting about what you have to offer on your squeeze page. The best part about setting things up this way is that it allows you to tap into the massive amounts of Traffic that Twitter receives in a more permanent way than just growing a list of followers on the network.

When it comes to improving your marketing results on Twitter, the most important thing you can do is always provide valuable content. In fact, providing information that has value is one of the best ways to grab attention and gain more followers.
It could be something as basic as a famous quote or a tip on how to improve one's life. People are more likely to follow somebody who has some helpful words and can be converted to customers once a bond has been established in the community. You can leave your links in some posts where they'll look good, so followers can find out what you're offering. Always remember that spamming the link in each post can annoy people and they can unfollow you just as fast as they followed you.

- Hashtags

Twitter has always been Hashtag king. There's the trending hashtags section visible from the home page to help you join in-the-moment, live conversations. Hashtags such as day-related #mondaymotivation or #fridayfeeling are predictable so schedule relevant content for these days. Additionally, you can find relevant events in Twitter Analytics along with their potential reach from earlier years. Observe what is currently trending on Twitter and include the hashtags in your post where applicable. Of course, they will have to match your tweet, but having a popular hashtag can send your post trending and can be re-tweeted by others, which is what it's all about. Using this as a marketing strategy can increase your post's viewership apart from those who are following you. If one gets off the ground, create another one that has the same tag and add a link. Many people will gain access to your promotion if you are still popular. Avoid following thousands of people with the prospect of arousing interest. Instead, you'll want to increase the number of people beating a trail down your promotional path and to accomplish this, you have to grab attention with the proper use of hashtags.

- Don't overuse links

On a regular basis, you can post a link to your blog or product site, but don't get carried away. People who pepper their posts with marketing links will soon lose their following as tons of sales pitch choking up their page irritates people. They don't want to wade through all that to find interesting posts. They will just block you and you're finished. Get attention through interesting posts and insert your links at random to get more chance of success. Instead of just sharing your blog post and its web URL, share the content of the blog post in small chunks of information. Segment the blog post in bullet points into actionable tips, then encourage people to check out the other tips on your blog.

- Giveaways

Offering some giveaway or holding a contest that will require people to follow you is a smart way of boosting the number of those linking to you. Be courteous enough to respond to those who have contacted you or replied to your tweets. They are prospective clients so don't waste time in getting back to them. Twitter is a potential goldmine if you know how to use it. Don't come off as a spammer who isn't concerned with what people think. Remember that you are building a community of interested followers. Be active online, re-tweet other posts, reply to people but don't overdo the links and the sales pitch.

Many types of businesses these days rely on the power of social media as an effective marketing tool. One of the more popular social media sites is Twitter, which is known for uniting an immense number of individuals in one enormous online community. With some Twitter marketing skills, you can advertise your website, products and/or services in less time at a very low cost and here are a few ways to do that.

- Use good keywords

Search your niche for important keywords and choose the ones which you can seamlessly include in your bio. The chosen keywords should look natural. If keywords or phrases are hard to find for that purpose, choose words that are associated with your niche or subjects to discuss. Construct your sentences in relation to these words. One possibility is to add in two of these words as you talk about your work experience or special skills. Links to your videos or articles should have a sentence or phrase that serves as an introduction for them. It can describe a solution to your target's long-standing problem. Use a personal tone, not a sales pitch, in your technique. Add the keyword that you used in your video or article into your tweet but don't make it sound like you're selling something. Nothing can make you lose your followers faster than this.

- Ask for re-tweets

Don't be ashamed to ask for re-tweets. You hear this marketing tip a lot, but many don't put it into practice. Don't expect your followers to automatically re-tweet your message no matter how great they appreciate them. Simply request them to re-tweet any of your posts that they think will be helpful or interesting.

- Use inspiration

Twitter users who frequently post words that empower or encourage people to face life's challenges attract a large share of Twitter traffic. Let's say for instance that you are campaigning for a consulting company for small scale businesses. Share a couple of amazing quotes that will drive small business owners to push harder to reach their goal. You can also post advice on how to succeed in their undertakings. They would definitely want to 'follow' you to learn more. Inspirational content preparation takes purposeful planning and should include a mix of images, GIFs and videos. You could share quotes, infographics or any other information that will motivate, inspire, informs, educate, and entertain your audience. Ask important engaging questions, share your success, lessons, news and 3rd party content.

- Take a Stand

Many people are inclined to 'follow' people who post daring statements. Don't be afraid to disagree with the opinion if you have to. However, you can present your opposition without using strong words as they can offend your followers and hurt the brand, you're trying hard to promote.

- Connect

Even if you are using your Twitter account to promote your brand, nothing should prevent you from sharing your ideas, hopes, and dreams with your followers to allow them to connect with you in a more personal manner. You can gain their trust as they get to know the real you. You can apply all the techniques described above or maybe some of them that will fit your promotional strategies. Bear in mind that constant practice of these techniques can increase your chances of succeeding in the future.

Now that you are getting the hang of marketing on Twitter let's talk about how you can get your tweets to spread even further thereby increasing your chance of connecting with more people to grow your following. Re-tweeting is a common practice on Twitter, which I'm sure you have noticed by now. It's where you re-post someone else's tweet that you like, and you think your followers will like. With this method, you take the original twitter message someone else has posted and rebroadcast that same message to your followers. Whenever you are broadcasting a message, you should definitely give credit to the original poster. I know at first it may sound like this will only be good for the original tweeter, but retweeting can actually benefit you just as much if not more and here are some very good reasons why you should start re-tweeting right away. Besides sharing engaging questions and fostering conversation, Twitter is a great way to build a network. Twitter chats have become popular so it's a good time to join or start your own chat. Be sure to monitor conversations and thank people for engaging with you. This can be a lot of work and it can be easy to miss an opportunity to engage so consider using the Communit software.

There's the underused, yet powerful search feature that lets you discover, listen and engage with topics of interest. Make use of Twitter List to stay connected with various groups of people.

- It provides value

When you provide value to your followers, you make them happy! You are also more likely to attract followers. Providing quality content is always a great way to build your business no matter what platform you use.

- It benefits your brand

If you point a reader to a source of good information that is truly relevant and beneficial to them, the amount of trust that they have in you will increase.

- It builds relationships

Retweeting someone else's content is an act of kindness, and for the most part bloggers like to return the favor. You shouldn't expect someone to re-tweet your content just because you retweet theirs. Just keep in mind that your chance of being on the other end of a re-tweet increases as you retweet. Retweeting is all about providing value to your followers so if you want others to retweet your post then you want to make sure that you are providing them with quality content worth tweeting about. The bottom line is retweeting is a great way to add quality and value to your Twitter page. If done right, retweeting can help you educate your followers, build your personal brand, increase future traffic, and connect you to other great people in your niche. Just be careful if you use it incorrectly, retweeting can actually hurt your personal brand and future traffic. You want to treat your followers like gold. Don't ever send them to inappropriate websites or spam them with one sales pitch after another.

Whether you want to generate more traffic to your site or you want to increase your social relationships, Twitting is a fun and exciting activity that you can quickly master and use to achieve your goals. We already know that Twitter is all about making connections. Some people send tweets regularly (every day) and others only a few times a week. Since you are planning on using Twitter as a marketing tool chances are you are going to be spending a lot of time managing your campaigns. Thankfully there are a wide variety of tools you can use to make the job easier and more efficient.

Which leads us to our first tool, Tweet Deck
https://about.twitter.com/products/tweetdeck

TweetDeck is a free downloadable application that works from your desktop and connects to your twitter account. Its main benefits are that you can see the main Twitter time line, the mentions you get and your DM's all on the one screen.

This interface design makes it much easier to manage your Twittering. The other good things about it are you can control multiple Twitter accounts from it, re-tweet with one click and follow/unfollow – all from the one place. You can also see your Facebook timeline too!

Next, we have Social Oomph
https://www.socialoomph.com/

Social Oomph previously known as Tweet Later. This tool lets you schedule your tweets, auto-follow people who follow you and send them a DM (direct message) automatically and much more. They do offer a free service but there is also the option to upgrade for even more features. It allows you to schedule tweets to go out automatically at a time you set. This is great if you aren't able to send important tweets because you have other commitments. It only takes a few minutes to set up and you can use to automatically post your prepared tweets. This can be handy for business if you are preparing a product launch or an event such as a teleseminar/webinar and want to keep your followers up to date about it but don't want to be manually posting to Twitter. It gives you the option to auto-follow people who follow you and send them a DM at that time automatically. This is a great way to introduce yourself and make friends quickly. You can add a short message in the DM that goes "thanks for following me. I'm an expert in ABC so please let me know how I can help you." Just make sure your message doesn't go over 140 characters. You probably don't want to send them straight to your website or else they'll ignore your message because it sounds like a sales pitch.

Then you have your WordPress Plugins

If you are using WordPress for your blog, there are quite a few tools that you can use to automate your Twitter activities from inside your dashboard including:
The Official Twitter Widget. The official widget from Twitter was not designed for WordPress, however it is still a great option. It allows you to display tweets from a range of sources including your own feed, tweets you have favorites, tweets from

lists you have created, search queries, and collections. You can define the height of the widget and choose from either a light or dark color scheme. The widget contains a follow button to allow people to follow you on Twitter directly through your website. Get it here: https://twitter.com/settings/widgets (you must be logged into your Twitter account)
TweetThis plug-in - It will encourage your visitors to tweet your blog post. TweetThis also adds a Twitter link in every blog post you create plus gives you the ability to shorten your blog post URL to fit the 140-character limit. Get it here: https://wordpress.org/plugins/tweetthis/

Twitter Tools - This plug-in integrates your blog with Twitter by pulling all your tweets into the side bar of your blog. You can also use it to post new tweets from inside your WordPress blog. Get it here: https://wordpress.org/plugins/twitter-tools/

Lastly, we have Simple Twitter Tweets
It's a useful Twitter widget plugin that stores Tweets in your database so that your widget will not be blank if the Twitter API fails. The plugin allows you to display your profile avatar, and a follow button with follower count, underneath the widget. Get it here: https://wordpress.org/plugins/simple-twitter-tweets/
The list goes on. I could literally list hundreds of tools that work with Twitter and can help you interact with the platform more effectively. If you want to find more all you have to do is search online and you will find plenty of options to choose from. Better yet, ask your followers what their favorite apps are, and it will help your relationship grow!

What can you do with Twitter polls?
Now, why are so many people (including me) so excited about this new feature? The answer is simple: There are so many great possibilities with these Twitter polls, and they are easy and fun to use. To give you some ideas about what you can do with Twitter polls, here are some examples of how they already are used and some ideas about how you could use them:

There are endless options for engaging your audience with polls in sports.

1. Ask for the outcome of a Game or competition
2. Ask which player should play
3. Ask if the referee made the right decision
And much more.

The media always has a need for public opinions. Before elections, with controversial topics, with fun questions, and more. Public opinion now comes much more accessible – well at least restricted to the people on Twitter. But for a variety of questions, the Twitter crowd should give a pretty good idea of the public opinion.
4. Ask for opinions on popular and current questions
5. Ask who people would vote for

Organizers of events can engage their attendees. Often at events, a Hashtag is given for the event, and people tweet around the occasion. Poll organizers now can push activity and inspire a ton of conversation about the events – even long before the event starts:

6. Ask what a good topic for the event would be
7. Ask which venue to choose
8. Ask for the best date for your event
9. Ask who you should invite for speaker on a certain topic
10. Ask who was the best speaker
11. Ask for feedback on the organization of the event
12. Ask for content preferences
You can ask whether your audience wants a webinar or a video, an article or a podcast, an online course or an eBook.

13. Ask for content you should cover
You can also ask your audience which topics you should cover and what information they would love to get from you.

14. Ask for Product Feedback

15. Use polls to help your customer service. Ask what their favorite way is of getting in touch for inquiries.

16. Gather insights about your audience

You can use the polls to ask where your audience is located, when they are online or how they use Twitter.

17. Let the audience vote on your Twitter activity

What kind of tweets do they like: discussions, blog posts, news, ...

So far engagement on Twitter polls seems fairly strong compared to other tweets. Fun to use, easy to set up and easy to answer. The feature seems to agree very well with the fast-moving Twitter world.

Have Fun!

Developing a brand on Twitter is important, but if you're not careful, that brand could come with a bad reputation. So, what are the biggest Twitter dos and don'ts? Do register for a free account and now. Unfortunately, many new marketers put off registering for a free account. Yes, there are no guarantees that your Tweet messages will lead to increased traffic or income, but you won't know until you try. Don't send personal messages to prospective clients or site visitors. This is very unprofessional. If you're trying to sell a product, don't talk about how much fun you are having at a college party. Do create two separate accounts for personal and business use. You should also avoid sending personal messages to prospective clients. You can send private messages to your friends and family, but this can be a time-consuming process. Instead, create two separate accounts, as you will save time and there will be no confusion. Don't spam. Spam is a big violation on Twitter. You may find your account banned. If that wasn't bad enough, think about the consequences. Your name, website, and products may be attached to your messages, resulting in a bad reputation. Do use clever forms of advertising. Spamming is prohibited on Twitter, but advertisements are allowed in moderation. If you don't abuse the privilege, you will not find trouble. Even still, use clever forms of advertising. Instead of highlighting your services as a professional web content writer, ask readers to review your samples or give you input on your rates. Be sure to include a link. Don't pressure your followers to buy. Your followers are those who signed up to receive your Tweet updates. They chose to do so of their own free will; however, they can also choose to end these updates. That is why no pressure should be applied. Users don't want to feel used; therefore, use clever forms of advertising, as there is less pressure. Do include a link. When sending Twitter updates to followers, include a link. Don't over abuse links but use them to your advantage. Once again, it's important to be clever. Don't spam your followers with advertisements highlighting your writing service rates. Instead, answer the Twitter question of what you are doing. Your message could say "Writing articles for a client." Then, insert your link. You aren't soliciting business, but making it know you work for hire. Don't send late night tweets. It's no secret that home based and online workers work flexible hours. Yes, many may work the traditional 9-5, but others are up till the early morning hours. If you're one of those individuals, know that most are not on the same schedule. For that reason, avoid late night Tweets. Followers with mobile web alerts may be awoken from sleep. Do visit Search.Twitter.com and use @replies to your advantage. Many people Tweet about what they are doing, but others ask questions. With a search, you can find members who are looking to buy a product you may sell, looking for a service you may offer, or looking for advice you may offer on your website or blog. If so, send an @reply with a personal message and a link.

Millions of people are using Twitter to connect with each other all over the world, but when it comes to using it for marketing there are some things you should avoid doing because it will hinder your chances of success.

- Not using your picture as your profile avatar!

I'm sure you've seen it. Some users don't post their real picture. Admittedly, a cartoon picture, or a cheaply made company logos is better than no picture at all. But the best picture you can use if you want to make a good impression and get people to remember you is a photo of your face. When you post your own picture, it lets others know that you are real and that you're confident enough with what you do to let others see you. You want people to recognize you as a leader in your market and having a face to go with a name always helps. A nice smile never hurts either.

- Automatically sending the wrong type of direct message through an AutoDM.

We talked about using the tool Future Tweets that automatically sends messages to people who follow you. What we didn't talk about was sending the wrong type of message with this tool and how it can lose you followers. Direct messages can be seen as impersonal and pushy when they aren't written properly. If you decide to use a tool that automatically send messages to your new followers keep it simple and friendly. A message saying 'thanks for following me' is fine, but sending automated messages promoting your business or product is not a good idea and most instances people will click the unfollow button right away.

- Trying to build a huge following before you have done some tweeting.

People will not be interested in following you when they click on your Twitter page to see what you've got and notice you don't have much. You need to have tweeted more than, "Trying to figure this Twitter out" and "I think I've got it figured out now." If you don't know what to say, try "retweeting" (RT) some other peoples' tweets that that are related to your niche. Read what other people are tweeting about and reply to them, this will help start up a conversation. Talk about market related news, what you're doing on your business right now. That will give you several tweets to get the ball rolling.

- Tweeting promotion after promotion.

Yes, you're using Twitter to promote your business, but posting one offer after another will only cause people to 'unfollow' you. When people look at your timeline and notice that you aren't posting anything of value to them, they will quickly move on. There are millions of Twitters to follow, why should they follow you when you're only tweeting about promotions? Remember this basic rule of sales "people want to know what's in it for me"? Always remember, Twitter is a social network filled with real people and you have to keep that in mind before you post a tweet. When you are using Twitter for marketing you must learn how to communicate and build good relationships with your followers before you start sending them promotions. Even if you already have a good list of leads, it is still not a good idea to barrage them with promotions. As we have talked about before, promotional tweets should be sent only in limited numbers. These are just a few of the more common mistakes committed by new and old tweeters alike. Take note of them and don't make the same mistakes.

Tweeting too often

The simple truth is that people who are following you are interested in you – but they're not THAT interested in you! I see some people Tweeting every few minutes – in many cases it's all automated and just links to websites. If people think you are appearing on their homepage too much – and it's not relevant to them – they will unfollow you! Don't make the mistake of tweeting too often.

Not tweeting enough

The other extreme of course is people who don't tweet enough.
I'm sure you will agree that it's kind of hard to show much interest in someone who last tweeted 6 months ago. Make it your goal to tweet a couple of times a day. Some days you will of course tweet more and other days you will tweet less. The exact numbers don't really matter but it's important to ensure that you tweet on a regular basis.

Always selling

Another one of the most common mistakes which I see people making on a regular basis on Twitter is always selling stuff, always promoting their websites etc. Let's face it – you wouldn't switch on a TV and watch a channel which only shows adverts all day long – so don't do exactly that on Twitter. People follow you because they are interested in you. They want to know about you and gain useful information about the niche you are in. Of course, it's ok to sell sometimes (let's face it, there's little point in using Twitter for business if you NEVER promote anything) but don't make the mistake of doing it all the time.

Making Tweets – The Right Way!

By far and away the best piece of advice I can give on Twitter is to post great information. What are your followers interested in? What information do they want to know? What are their questions? What motivates them? Why are they following you? I always say to people – "give your followers a reason to continue following you!" This might be by posting links to information and products you think they will be interested in. It could be by posting anecdotal stories about things which are happening to you – or answering people's questions about the niche, giving advice, talking to people. Make sure your Tweets aren't just a series of promotions. Yes, you can promote – but you also need to point people in the direction of free content, show off your knowledge and show off your passion.

Let's say your primary niche is internet marketers. Your followers are people who want to learn about internet marketing – people who want to build an online business or make more money online. They are following you because they want to learn from you and they are looking at you as an authority source.

Examples of Tweets you might make are on the following pages...

8am: Good morning Twitterers, how are you today? Fine day here in the UK so heading outside to work in the garden
^ This is good because it makes you seem personable. You are asking your followers how they are – and you are revealing a little bit about what you're up to. People love to know a little about your personal life!

9am: Just read a very interesting blog post by @username about how to increase your subscriber numbers. LINK TO BLOG POST ^ This is a good post to make because you are sharing useful information with others. By including the blog authors Twitter account in the tweet, it also lets the other person know that you have just promoted their blog for them. People really appreciate this because essentially you are promoting their business for them – and over time you will find that people start doing the same thing back to you.

10am: Does anyone have any shopping cart software they could recommend?
^ Encouraging other people to chip in with their own ideas/opinions/recommendations etc. is a great idea because it makes your followers feel involved. If someone tweets you to answer your question you can then thank them for doing so and that starts to build up a relationship with them.

11am: @username You could try xyz. Always worked for me ⏹
^ People ask questions all the time on Twitter, so when you see someone asking something and you can help them make sure you do so!

12am: @username That's a great idea – thanks for the share.
^ If you see one of your followers sharing some great information, thank them for doing so. You could even chip in with your own idea and add a little something to what they were saying.

1pm: RT @username Their original Tweet here
^ A re-tweet is when you see something you found useful/interesting and you want it to appear on your own profile for your followers to see. By re-tweeting something you are not only sharing good information with your followers, but you are also building a relationship with the person who made the original tweet. They will see that you have re-tweeted their tweet and they will usually thank you for it because effectively it is free advertising for them.

2pm: My new product, Bring You're a-Game, has just gone live! Check it out at LINK HERE
^ All that other stuff is great, but you ARE going to want to promote stuff from time to time – and there's absolutely nothing wrong in doing so providing that you aren't doing it ALL the time. Just make sure that what you are promoting will actually be interesting to your followers.

IT'S OKAY TO JUMP INTO A CONVERSATION

In addition to regular ole tweets, Twitter is full of conversations among people. If you follow two people and see they have a conversation going that sounds interested, don't be shy! Just @ them both so they both see what you're saying. **That's the equivalent of...** walking by two people at a party talking about your favorite Italina restaurant. And then you jump in with a "Excuse me. I overheard you talking about my favorite restaurant. I LOVE that place!" Of course, someone could be all snotty and not respond back but who cares? It's worked for me in connecting with people more often than it's not. When this tactic would really suck is when someone is having a super serious conversation and you jump in with "hi guys!" Be smart. Of course, we could argue deep convos should be taken elsewhere but let's just not go there.

SPEAK OFF THE TOP OF YOUR MIND (WITHIN REASON)

Whether it's an opinion, an observation or just a random thought, tweet it! While no one wants to read EVERY little thought that crosses your mind during the day, I've found that I get the most responses when I just let it out.

That's the equivalent of... seeing some of your friends at a party and telling them what's been happenin'. For example, the other day I tweeted this ridiculousness, "Just realized I forgot to put on deodorant. Thank God I work from home." One silly (and kind of embarrassing) tweet like that had people responding to me laughing, saying that happens to them all the time, etc. Why is that important? Because we made a connection and interacted like friends would, even if it was at the expense of my armpits. Use this tip at your own discretion- you may never ever ever want to divulge information about forgetting deodorant. You may never want to tell your followers that you're craving pizza or that your dog just peed on the carpet (and if you're a business, I'd be conservative in tweeting like this). BUT I've gotten the most laughs and interaction from the silly stuff.

Here's a daily checklist to help you get started in unlocking the power of Twitter.

- Share or schedule 10 Post Daily

- Follow 50 People

- Check Twitter for Conversations and Respond to them

- Use Trending Hashtags to conduct in-the-moment Tweets

- Check Twitter Lists to take part in Specific Conversations

- Check Twitter List of Influencers and comment on 10 Blog Posts

- Scroll Home Page

- Browse over DM and reply to urgent ones

- Browse your feed and like or retweet 10 random posts

How to Increase Your Twitter Followers

FOLLOW as many people as you can. Now, you don't want to follow anyone & everyone – you only want to follow people you want to engage with. Why? Because this a great way to get onto their radars – many of the people you want to talk to will follow you back & this is how you begin building a relationship with them. Go ahead and follow 2,000 people. If you follow them, you give them the opportunity to follow you back.

- DO follow as many people as Twitter allows. As you approach 2,000 followers, Twitter will continue raising the bar of how many people you can follow. I don't know the exact rule, but it's something to do with the ratio of people you follow (following) to people who follow you (followers).
- DON'T overthink it. You aren't marrying your followers, so don't spend too long agonizing over whether or not you want to follow someone.
- DON'T spend a lot of time selecting followers. They will not all follow you back, and in a later step you will be unfollowing people to make room to follow new people.

OK now that you know you should follow 2,000 people, you want to be sure you are following the right people. Who are the right people? That depends on who you want to connect with online. Are you selling something to a certain group? Are you trying to build an audience for your blog? Are you looking to discuss a specific topic? Keep in mind the "purpose" of your twitter presence.

Where do you find the right people? You look at their followers. While you're looking around, identify individuals whose followers look like your "perfect" followers. I like to save these people to a Twitter list called "copy followers" that I mark as private and then I FOLLOW THEIR FOLLOWERS. That's it! Just go down their list of followers and start following each of them.

REMOVE! COPY! ADD! REMOVE People you follow who don't follow you back. Why? Once you are following 2,000, you only want to stay connected with the people who follow you back. Why? Then you have the opportunity to follow new people who may want to build a relationship with you. You want to remove your Non-Followers (the people who don't follow you).

Statusbrew has an awesome app that you can try for free on your Phone. The benefit to this tool is that you can QUICKLY remove non-followers and copy new followers of someone else's. You could perform these tasks using Twitter, but it will be a slow & tedious job. If you want to grow your Twitter following, don't obsess over who to follow & unfollow. Just do it!

Conclusion

Twitter is a great way of marketing online but ONLY if you use it in the correct way.

Take the time at the beginning to set up your profile in full and get it looking as good as you possibly can.

When you're ready to get some followers, use the 'follow them' and they will follow you back' method we talked about earlier to generate your first few hundred subscribers.

Remember also to promote your Twitter account in other places too. Include a link to it on any other places you can think of – other social networking sites, forums that you participate in, blogs etc.

From there it's simply a case of tweeting good information. Doing so will make your followers responsive AND you'll find that you start generating new followers without actively going out there and looking for them yourself.

Tweet good information. Talk to people (that is absolutely crucial) and concentrate on building relationships with your followers. You can sell too but make sure you don't do it all the time.

Timing is key too. Try to tweet regularly but not so often that it takes over your life and annoys the hell out of your followers!

If you take on board the advice given in this report, you should be well on your way to generating extra profits and boosting your business through Twitter. …. So happy tweeting!

PINTEREST

    If you're a marketer and you're not on Pinterest, then you're missing out on one of the biggest and the most flexible/powerful platforms out there. Pinterest may not be quite as big as Facebook in terms of pure users but it's actually not as far behind as you might think. What's more, it has a ton of unique features that present excellent opportunities for the savvy marketer.

The main problem that brands seem to have when it comes to Pinterest is that they don't see how they can get it to relate to them. Pinterest is very visual and creative, it's made up of images that people pin to their 'boards' and that others can then comment on or 're-pin'. Thus, it clearly lends itself to companies that have an artistic, trendy, stylish or visual side. But how can this possibly be useful for a company that sells life insurance? Or for a blogger who is promoting the 'work online' lifestyle?

And seeing as Facebook and Twitter are so much bigger, does it really matter? Well the first thing you should get out of your head is the idea that Pinterest isn't that big. In fact, Pinterest currently has 100 million users which is really pretty massive – and a subset of the market that you just can't ignore. Also interesting is that 85% of those 100 million users are female. This is quite unique for any social network and provides you with a great way to reach a female audience – something that a lot of blogs and brands could stand to do a little more effectively. 42% of all adult women in the US use Pinterest which is massive – and actually 13% of males do which is still rather significant.

And while Pinterest has a ton of users, it also has the advantage of being a platform that visitors can enjoy without signing up. That means that your potential reach is in fact much larger than you might at first have thought. Pinterest is also one of the fastest growing platforms and is expected to acquire another 47.5 million users in 2019. So, you need to be on Pinterest and this is especially true once you realize that there are plenty of ways you can succeed on the platform even if your niche isn't terribly creative or visual.

Over the course of this chapter we'll look at some more creative and imaginative approaches that you can take to your Pinterest marketing and we'll see how many other brands have managed to take the network by storm. Better yet, you'll find that Pinterest is actually one of the easiest social networks to manage and maintain. The amount of time and money you'll invest here is miniscule, and especially when compared with the amount you stand to gain. This is a very high ROI and it demands your attention!

With that in mind, this chapter is going to act as your comprehensive guide to mastering Pinterest. By the end, you'll know everything you need to know to get set up and to start building a massive audience. What's more, we'll go over some advanced strategies and techniques you can employ to get one step ahead of the competition and to accelerate your growth trajectory. You'll be armed with unrivalled knowledge of the platform and you'll be poised and ready to become a real force to be reckoned with on the platform.

Essentially, Pinterest works by allowing you to create 'mood boards. Anyone who has done an art course will be familiar with this term. For everyone else, a mood board is essentially a collage made up of images and other materials that you've found on the web. This lets you collect images and notes from anywhere online and to categorize them in one spot as a 'board'. These boards can then be shared by other users and brands and you can follow either individual boards or users if you'd like to see more that they've created or collected.

To find images to pin to your boards, you can either browse other boards and then 'repin' the content you like, you can save images from the web and use social sharing buttons, or you can create your own content to upload to the site. You can use the inbuilt search tools in Pinterest to search for users, for boards or for specific items. If you want to see images of 'futuristic fonts' for instance, then you can search for that string and you'll be provided with a ton of images that other people and brands have pinned. Images have hashtags on them which describe their content, and this then helps you when you're searching for more content.

The key difference that Pinterest has when compared to something like Facebook then, is that the social aspect is actually not at the forefront. You can keep the boards you create as 'private' if you like and this then means that no one else will see them. This means you can use it simply to collect ideas for your own projects or for your general inspiration – and CEO Ben Silbermann actually describes the tool as a 'catalogue of ideas' rather than a social network. His hope is that it can be used to inspire to people to, in his words, 'go do that thing'.

Once you're following a number of boards and users, you'll also be able to see pins that your contacts have pinned or commented on. You'll also see images based on similar pins you have uploaded. This creates a 'homefeed' of sorts that you can browse just to find images you might find interesting or inspiring, or to see what your friends are up to.

Like any social network, Pinterest also offers a plethora of social elements. Other than using it to browse different users' content and edit it, it can also allow you to post comments on the pins you like (or don't like!), or to re-pin the content you enjoy and thereby share it with your own network. It's also possible to invite people to edit your boards and to set them up to be informed every time you add a new pin to it. This is a great feature for working on collaborative projects for instance and the boards are known as 'group boards.

There are many more features to Pinterest than this. In fact, even if you have been using Pinterest for a while there's a very good chance that you won't have seen everything it has to offer and that you won't know all the different things you can do with the platform. Further in this chapter, we'll be looking at some of those more advanced features in more detail and seeing how you can utilize them for marketing benefits.

There are many common ways that Pinterest gets used. Here are just a few:

1. Collecting images that you find appealing/inspiring
2. Collating ideas and inspiration for a new web design/app
3. Getting ideas for interior design
4. Browsing products and 'window shopping'
5. Putting together inspirational images to get you into the gym (moves, 'goal physiques' etc.)
6. Staying updated with your favorite brand in a more visual manner

7. Looking at fashion and outfit ideas for clothes
8. Researching tattoo ideas
   And much more

Marketing With Pinterest

Now you know the basics of how Pinterest works, it's time to look at how this can be used by marketers and why Pinterest is such a powerful tool beyond just being a big platform to reach a large audience.

What features in particular make Pinterest a good choice for your business? How do you go about using it to promote your website or company?

As mentioned, a lot of people will use Pinterest primarily for researching ideas and getting inspiration. If they enjoy interior design, graphic design, fashion or fitness, they'll likely have lots of boards relating to that topic. What's more, they'll probably be following some other boards created by big brands in those areas.

As a brand, your objective is to be 'one of those brands' that people follow and to use this as a prime opportunity to show off your products, your services and your website so that you get more visitors and more business.

This is particularly easy if you should happen to work in one of the industries that is particularly popular on Instagram. If you create wedding decorations for instance, then all you need to do is to create a board dedicated to these and then let people pin the items they find there or just browse your site for ideas. The more people you can get to follow you, the more people will see your products, will be exposed to your brand and will likely buy your items. This ultimately means you can get a lot of traffic and engagement from a well-thought-out Pinterest board.

What will help here is the ability to easily add links to your website and specific articles and blog posts. If you choose to 'Pin from the Web', you can then type in an URL and select an image from that website to go along with it. Under the pin, it will then say, 'Pinned from' and you can click that to follow through to the blog post or article where it was originally posted. This means that people can follow your boards to stay up-to-date with your new articles and blog posts if they want as well, which they may choose to do if Pinterest is their preferred platform.

Beyond the basic features, there are also some more advanced options and tools on Pinterest that are going to be especially useful for marketers.

One example is 'Article Rich Pins'. These have been around since September 2013 and they basically take the central concept of posting links to blogs and articles and build on it. These allow you to share links as you already could, but the additional advantage is that you can add extra information about the article – such as the title, the site name, the description and the author. This makes your blog and article links considerably more appealing and it encourages people to sign up automatically.

Article rich pins are actually just one of the advance types of 'rich pins' available for marketers and we'll be looking at more in further detail later in this chapter. Another relatively new and big feature of Pinterest that is particularly interesting for marketers is the 'buyable pins' tool. This was introduced relatively recently so not every marketer is making full use of it. As the name suggests, buyable pins are pins showing products that are for sale. So, if you should be browsing the site and see an item of clothing, a desktop accessory, or maybe a piece of furniture that you like, then you can simply click to buy it. In the iPad and iPhone apps, the 'Pin It' button is now accompanied by a 'Buy It' button that lets users immediately buy the products they're interested in. By the end of the very first month, there were already 2 million of these pins on the site.

Pinterest has long been popular as a tool for 'window shopping'. When users are looking through other brand boards because they're looking for ideas for wedding decorations, things to wear or things to decorate their house with, they will often then follow the links to buy the products, or later look up the product.

But now with buyable pins, they can buy the product straight through Pinterest itself. This turns your Pinterest board into an ecommerce store, essentially meaning that anything on your site can now be easily bought. If you imagine that someone has taken a lot of time amassing a selection of items, they find inspiring for their wedding, this means they can now eventually whittle that selection down just to the things they want and click 'buy'. This creates the barrier to sale and makes it a much thinner line between 'discovery' and sale. It's very simple and easy and it's a very tempting new option for businesses.

Finally, Pinterest also provides a large amount of analytics data. To get access to this you'll need to convert your personal account to a 'business account' and at the same time, you'll need to verify your account. From there, you'll then be able to see what pins are getting pinned from your website or blog. This in turn lets you see which content is really performing well and engaging your audience.

That's right, if you want to take full advantage of the analytics features on Pinterest, then you need to upgrade to a business account. And there are other advantages of making this switch too.

Can you promote your blog or business with a personal account? Of course, you can: to an extent. But there are some considerable advantages of making the switch.

For starters, Pinterest actually requires you to make your Pinterest account a business one if you intend on using it to profit. While it's unlikely they'll clamp down on you for posting links to your website, you should switch if you want to tow the official line.

Their statement on the matter is:

"If you're using Pinterest as part of how you make a living, whether by driving traffic to a blog that makes you some money or to build your personal brand to find customers for your products or services, you should sign up for a business account and agree to our Business Terms of Service."

From here, you'll then be able to display your company or brand name as the title of your Pinterest profile instead of your first and last name, you'll be able to get insider tips and strategies from Pinterest (they provide a lot of free educational materials) and you'll be able to verify your website. As mentioned, it's this latter step that enables you to see which of your photos and images are getting shared on Pinterest, getting repined and getting commented on.

Verifying your URL also has another benefit – it adds your hyperlink to the top of your profile. This now means that anyone who discovers your Pinterest account will now be able to quickly discover your website as well and that means more traffic, more ad clicks, more sales etc. Business accounts are also allowed to host contests through their Pinterest, which is something we'll be looking at further on in this book.

Your Strategy

At this point, you now have a full understanding of how Pinterest works, and you're set up with an account that looks the part and that should help more people to start finding the content you're creating.

Now all that's left is to actually begin marketing.

We've looked over most of the advantages of marketing on Pinterest already and we've seen how it lends itself well to promoting a website, blog or business. But now it's time to move away from the hypothetical and to start creating a business model that works.

Let's start with the basics. By looking at what makes any type of marketing strategy and any type of business successful. And the single answer here is value. If you want to engage your audience, if you want to build customers and fans and if you want to engender loyalty, then you need to be offering high quality value to achieve all those things. That means in other words, that you need to give people a concrete reason to want to spend time engaging with your brand.

The mistake that a lot of companies and marketers make on social media is simply to try and use it as a platform for promoting a product. They want to get direct sales, immediately and they're trying to reach a broader audience by doing this through social media. You'll see this when you follow a company on Twitter that does nothing but talk about its products or services:

"Try out our latest products today!"
"Want to save time in the office? Our productivity tools are just for you!"
"Hurry while stocks last!"

The equivalent on Pinterest is simply to post images from articles with no rhyme or reason, or to just post images of the same product over and over hoping someone will notice it. This is unfortunately an entirely incorrect approach and social media just doesn't lend itself to that kind of promotion. Why? Because you need people to want to follow you on social media. And if all you're doing is posting about your company then you're really not going to give anyone a chance to do that. Would you follow a social media profile that only ever tried to sell its products to you? Or would you quickly get bored and unsubscribe?
Instead, you need to think like the top brands on Pinterest and offer the kind of service that people are looking for on the platform: inspiration, ideas and lifehacks.

The ideal type of company for Pinterest is a company that sells wedding decorations, or perhaps that prints wedding invitations. You can then create a Pinterest board that will share images of wedding decorations – both involving your own products and using other products. Make sure that the ideas are unique and interesting, that they provide style and elegance on a budget and that they offer the kinds of ideas that your followers might not have come up with themselves. This way, you give them an actual reason to follow you – because they're learning!

Likewise, you might create a Pinterest board about 'battlestations' if you sell computer parts. Battlestations are essentially PC set-ups for gamers that are designed to look cool with lots of glowing parts and large dual monitor set-ups. Sell cupboards? Then you could create a board about organizational life hacks. Sell cooking ingredients? Then share pins of great meals and desserts and discuss the ingredients and the procedure in the comment's underneath.

In any of these cases, you're giving people a reason to follow you on Pinterest because you're offering value in the form of ideas, inspiration or just aesthetic beauty.

If you're selling a physical product and especially something that looks beautiful or that has a 'chic' appeal, then you'll find that Pinterest is the perfect fit for your business. But what if you sell insurance? What if you sell eBooks about making money through day trading? What if your niche isn't something that appeals to hipsters? How do you make this work on Pinterest?

The answer is that you need to go a little bit deeper and think about 'lifestyle' and about 'value proposition'. In terms of lifestyle, it's pertinent to consider that every product or service that you sell, will ultimately support some kind of lifestyle and will appeal to a certain type of person. Fitness eBooks for instance appeal to people who like working out and who want to be in better shape. The 'fitness lifestyle' is an inspiring and visual concept that you can portray with pictures of people jogging on the beach listening to an MP3 player, or with pictures of people working out outdoors.

Likewise, if you sell holiday insurance, then the lifestyle is the 'travelling' lifestyle. You can post images of beautiful foreign destinations, or you can have boards outlining things to do in particular places. 'Value proposition' meanwhile refers to the value that your product or service really offers beyond the sum of its parts. The old saying goes that you 'don't sell hats, you sell warm heads'. What this means, is that the true value of the hat is in its ability to keep your head warm. So, if you can't post pictures of your 'hat' then you can always post pictures of your 'warm head'.

What is the value proposition of life insurance? Simple: it's keeping your family happy and safe after you're gone and it's looking after finances. As such then, your board doesn't need to include images of life insurance policies (the hat) but instead should include pictures of happy families enjoying days out together and doing fun things (the warm head). Your board could just be designed to give people that 'warm fuzzy feeling' by showing people having a great time, or it could be used to provide tips and ideas: how about ideas for things for people to do together as a family on a budget. Maybe it could be filled with pictures that humorously satirize the nature of the modern family?

Likewise, if your blog is about SEO and digital marketing, then your value proposition is business success, wealth and the feeling of accomplishment that comes from making it big online. Perhaps it's also the freedom that you gain when you work for yourself and aren't restrained to work in an office with a boss leaning over your shoulder. To demonstrate this in a Pinterest board, you could show images of people working in exciting locations like huge libraries, or on the beach in a hammock. Likewise, you could show people in suits looking successful and well-dressed thanks to the money they managed to earn online.

The key either way here, is to come up with themes for your boards that deliver real value and purpose for Pinterest users while remaining 'on topic'. Don't just randomly repin pictures that vaguely relate, don't just promote your products and don't just post your articles randomly. If you do that you won't be providing value and you won't grow your viewership.

Think of your Pinterest profile almost like a service or a product in itself. The ideal scenario is that people will end up looking forward to checking out your pins or that they may even become reliant on your boards. They should be disappointed if ever your board gets taken down and the board should almost be able to exist on its own, as a separate entity from your business.

Selling Through Your Images

This still leaves us with one problem though.

If your board is about great interior design ideas and your company sells furniture and decorative items, then it's going to be very easy for you to include images of your products that people can click through to buy.

But if you sell life insurance and your board is about 'fun family days out' then you still won't be able to easily sell directly through the board. So how do you make sales from that?

On the whole, your objective here is not going to be to sell directly. Instead, the aim will be to raise awareness for your brand and to build trust and authority. The hope is that your audience will come to think of you as an expert on the subject of families and life insurance and as such, they will follow your links when they do want to find out more about getting a policy. This of course is not as direct a way to sell but in the long term it can actually be a lot more effective as you're building a long-term relationship and as you're establishing yourself as a thought leader in your field.

At the same time, you need to think about the comments that you're adding to your pictures. This is your opportunity to directly link the image back to your site and to promote your product. For instance, if you're uploading images of people doing home workouts to provide inspiration and ideas to your followers, then you can sell through those images by adding a note at the bottom explaining that they can find more similar moves in your eBook at THIS link.

The great thing about Pinterest is that it really does leverage the viral power of social networks. If your board is really delivering great value, then this fact alone will be enough to ensure that it grows naturally. People will repin your pins, they will comment, and they will discover what you're posting through the search button. If you're offering new content, if you're staying on topic and if you're providing real value by offering a genuine service of some kind, then people will gradually gravitate towards your brand and you'll build your following.

But that is not to say that there aren't also other things you can do to further accelerate your progress. Here are some of the ways you can grow your following more quickly:

Post Regularly: The more regularly you post, the more often your images will be found in searches. At the same time, they'll also come up in home feeds more often, which means other users will be more likely to repin them and thereby share them with their audiences giving you more exposure.

3 Simple Strategies for Marketing on Pinterest: Pinterest is a pin-board-style social network that connects everyone through things that people find interesting. The social website allows its users to create, manage and browse other pin-boards and re-pin or like posts. Not only that, but the site also allows users to share the 'pins' on other social sites such as Facebook and Twitter.

Being referred to as one of the swiftly growing social networks, Pinterest is indeed becoming a social media platform for online marketing opportunities. Moreover, many are not aware that it is not only a photo sharing site but a video sharing site as well. Moreover, the social site has already added Video platform that contributed to the growth of the site. To fully utilize the advantages of Pinterest, below are the three tips for marketing on Pinterest that marketers can follow.

Create a complete profile:

With the Video platform, pinners can now upload and customize video thumbnails. To do so, one must select an image that would catch the audience' attention at the same time appropriate for the video uploaded. Moreover, Pinterest allows users to create a few "pin-boards." A marketer may choose to post videos on separate pin-boards and place a creative description rather than titling "videos". Besides, do not leave the description field blank upon uploading a video. Besides the eye-catching thumbnail, most people would like read descriptions to know if it's worth to watch. Make sure always to describe what the video is about.

The pinners browse and pin their interest on a daily basis, and most do it every hour. Clearly, they can't be stuck on watching videos that are too long and, in turn, bore them. It is essential to post videos of reasonable length to ensure that Pinners will watch it from beginning till end. However, there are exceptions to that rule. Demo or do-it-yourself videos can be reasonably long since it gives instructions that people find helpful.

Include the Pin button to pin images that are interesting:

This is a simple way to connect with other Pinners or business pin-boards. First it gives a link to a person's or company's Pinterest account. Second, Pinterest follows button allows users to follow another user. Third, it enables users to interact with other users through comments and likes. Lastly, it tempts Pinners to re-pin a post. Thus, it increases marketing opportunities. Besides asking and allowing others to follow and re-pin videos, one should also re-pin other user's videos. In fact, re-pinning helps Pinners build their network of followers. However, it is essential to choose the ones to follow and re-pin. A good way is to find influential people in the same industry and reach out by following them and re-pinning appropriate videos.

Create a specific Pinterest video Campaign:

There are brands that have started creating video campaigns on Pinterest that encourages re-pinning their posts. Some even created a contest to submit a photo about certain topics. It is an effective marketing strategy that helps increase brand awareness just through pinning.

Choose Your Tags Careful: As on Twitter, choosing the right hashtags is one of the most important ingredients when it comes to gaining maximum exposure for your images. The tags will dictate which searches bring up your images and this means that they'll be directly responsible for the number of people finding your brand. When choosing your tags, make sure that you think about the types of things that commonly get searched for on the platform. Remember the kinds of things people use Pinterest for and remember that the audience is 85% female. Remember too that people are looking for images. 'How to' isn't as applicable here ('life hack' is a more suitable string).

Write Comments: If you upload an image without any comment then you give it no context. This means you won't be getting the very most from it, simply because people won't know what you're trying to say with the image. If it's a bodyweight exercise, then explain how to do the exercise! If it's a decoration for the home, then explain how people can use it, what it's made from and where it can be bought. Make sure to link your brand to the image, otherwise people might just appreciate the image but never engage with your profile as the person who uploaded it!

Interact With Others: On social media, reciprocity is a very underrated tool. This is still a social network and therefore, it should be used as a communication tool. The more you talk to people, the more likely they will be to check out your profile and to look at your boards. So, make sure that you're interacting, following, repining and more. If nothing else, this helps to build good will as you'll be helping those users to promote themselves too!

Optimizing Your Blogger Outreach on Pinterest: Optimizing Your Blogger Outreach on Pinterest is the single most important action item on your to do list for today! How do you go about doing this? Where does one start? First off, know the category champions and see where your product or service fits in. The more popular categories are:
• Food & Drink
• DIY & Crafts
• Home Décor
• Women's Fashion

- Fitness
- Technology
- Inspirational Quotes
- Humor
- Travel

Next, it is important to know your audience and how they browse, how they shop and when they let their hair down. Did you know that the most pin traffic is generated on Saturday mornings and on work weekdays between 2 and 4pm? This tells you that your customers love to browse for inspiration over a cup of coffee during relaxation time.

Know the laws of attraction:

Are you aware that light images are 20 x more attractive to Pinterest users as compared to darker images, and that the best pixel size for this purpose is 736 x 1102.

Advertise your prices – people want to be drawn in! They want to buy your product and it's your job to help them do that by utilizing a few tips and tricks on Optimizing Your Blogger Outreach on Pinterest.

- Be authentic
- Be highly relevant
- Use links
- Be customer focused
- Have great content
- Visually engage your customer
- Be professional
- Be unique
- Own your niche
- Build relationships

Integrate Your Website: One of the most important ways for you to spread your brand across Pinterest and to get found by more people is to properly link your website and your Pinterest account. There are a few ways that you should do this.

One is by adding a link on your homepage to your Pinterest account. This way, someone who lands on your website for the first time and decides that they like your content, can decide that they want to follow you on social media as well and can then decide to check out your Pinterest and follow your account or your boards.

Another tip is to use 'Shareabolic' or a similar social sharing tool on your website. If you have a WordPress site, then these can be installed very easily, and they will then allow people to quickly and easily 'Pin' an article that they found interesting along with an image. This then means there will be more people sharing your images and you'll gain more exposure as a result.

How to Create a Pinterest Graphic: Using Pinterest can help a business get a good amount of traffic. But many people struggle to get pinners ever to click on their pins, let alone click through to their websites. If pinners bypass your pins altogether, Using Pinterest will end up being a poor strategy for your business. There are some ways to optimize your pins so that they gain more attention with pinners. A major factor is the graphic or image that you use. The image is the primary means for which people will become interested in exploring more about you. You need to make it stand out. The first aspect of a Pinterest graphic is its size. The key is to make it longer rather than wide. If you were to make a wide graphic, Pinterest would truncate it, and pinners won't be able to see the graphic, especially if there is any text on it.

Pinners scroll down by nature when using Pinterest. Therefore, the longer your pins, the longer they focus on them. This is especially true if you make each section of the pin something they want to see. Consider using color to make your graphics stand out. Experiment with different colors and even add some blends or gradients into the mix. You should try to split test based on colors. For instance, try a blue pin and a green pin at the same time to see if one is favored over the other. Add a significant number of supplemental images to your Pinterest graphics, but don't overdo it. The images should be relevant to the message you are trying to convey. Too much flash, however, will get pinners to bypass your graphics. Make sure you have the rights to use the graphics you include in your pins. Don't take this issue lightly as there are companies that are paid to monitor copyright infringement. It is a serious offense that is likely to cost you several thousands of dollars. If you find a website that claims royalty free access to images, make sure you know their claims policy. You want them to fight for you if it ever comes down to that. When using text, make sure you are consistent with your font selections. Each section can have a different font but try to keep to no more than two or three fonts. You want to ensure that the website you link to is relevant to what the graphic portrays. If not, you can expect to have your pins reported to Pinterest.

3 Methods For Driving Traffic From Pinterest: Did you know that Pinterest can be used to drive traffic to your website? Recent research indicates that it is growing rapidly as a tool to boost your social media presence and drive traffic. According to Shareaholic's Traffic Report, Pinterest drives more than three times the traffic of Google Plus, YouTube, LinkedIn, StumbleUpon, Reddit and Twitter combined. But in order to get that traffic, you have to use the right methods. Just pinning your content will not help. The most important things on Pinterest are the images themselves. So, make an extra effort to create compelling and irresistible images. Once that is taken care of, you can focus on how to drive traffic using Pinterest. Here are three actionable methods that can help you.

1. Add a Pin It Button to Your Website

The first thing you need to do is to add a Pin It button to your website that will appear on every piece of content having an image. You can do it just like you add any other social media buttons.
Doing this will help visitors to share your content on Pinterest that they find interesting. And when they do so, their followers will also see it and further share it. This way, your content will gain popularity and credibility.

2. Make Your Board Easily Searchable

Creating the board on Pinterest is not sufficient. You have to make it easily searchable. Name your board same as your website or blog name. Also add description, taglines and links that tell people what your blog and board are all about. It will also make it easier to find your board on Pinterest as well as search engines. But make sure you don't stuff your description with keywords just to rank higher. Keep in mind that, ranking in searches will be of no use if you turn off your potential visitors. If many businesses don't even fill out their board descriptions, how many of them do you think add keywords to their images? That's right. Not many. Adding keywords to your pin images gives them an extra push up on the search ranking with Pinterest and on search engines. To do this, simply change the name of the image to include meaningful keywords that someone might search for before you upload it.

3. Improve Engagement

You need to engage people to get traffic to your website. Regularly share images that are not only compelling but also invoking curiosity and interest in the viewers so that they click on it and go to your website.
Also do research on your followers' interests and the kind of images they like and share.
Recently Pinterest has introduced the feature of Rich Pin. You can use it to add descriptions and specific information to your images to tell people more about the content they link to.

You see, if used the smart way, Pinterest can be a great source of referral traffic. If you implement the methods described above, you can attract a lot of visitors to your website.
But make sure you post images that are highly specific and relevant to your niche. This will help them to rank in searches and they will engage more viewers.

Cross Pollinate: You should also make sure that you occasionally try to cross pollinate between your social media channels. If you have a very successful Twitter account for instance, then occasionally tweet about the 'inspiring boards' you're creating at Pinterest. Likewise, you can share your pins to Facebook for people to see. Do this occasionally to help grow all of your accounts at once.

Think About Pinterest When You Create Content: If you've heard of 'clickbait' then you'll know how a lot of website owners are now creating content specifically to encourage shares on Facebook. This is content that uses an obtuse title in order to make people curious and to encourage more clicks as a result. It's frustrating but it works and sites like Buzzfeed have built their business off the back of it.
So, the point is, that thinking about how you're going to share you content before you create it is a good move. The same goes for marketing on Pinterest. If you're going to make an article successful on Pinterest, then what does it need? Simple:

it needs a great image that will make the article more compelling (this will also help when other people share your images and your pages). Make sure that you are creating unique images for your site and that they're designed in such a way as to really sell the content of your article or blog post and to encourage people to follow the URL. Some things that can work well are tips that can be portrayed through a single image, memes or inspirational quotes. Note as well that certain images automatically attract more attention than others – we are psychologically hardwired for instance to notice pictures of faces!

6 Tips for Pinterest Marketing in Just Minutes a Day: Pinterest marketing can take too much time if you don't implement the right strategies. A comprehensive Pinterest marketing campaign can deliver amazing results with very little effort. Here are 6 tips to help you market on Pinterest in just minutes a day.

1. Repin Each Day For A Few Minutes

You should take at least three minutes each day to repin and curate to your Pinterest boards. Type in keywords for your niche in Pinterest search and based on your initial search, you will see additional search terms. Click on one of the words under the search bar and you'll be able to add them. This makes it easier for you to find the best content that you can share.

2. Schedule Pins

This is one of the best strategies to keep your account active during weekends. It is recommended that you do this for at least 5 minutes on Fridays after posting your daily pins. When Scheduling pins you can choose a number of tools including Tailwin, Buffer or Viralwoot to post images. Tailwind is a better option as it allows you to schedule pins through your browser extension.

3. Follow Pinners In Your Industry Or Niche

To ensure a successful Pinterest marketing campaign, you need to follow relevant pinners in your industry or niche. Ensure that you follow 3 to 5 pinners every day. But you should avoid following just anyone. Ensure that you review the profile of a pinner before following him/her. Spare sometime in the course of the day (at least 5 minutes) to search for new pinners.

4. Comment On A Pin Every Day

Always check out for relevant pins you can comment each day. You can like many pins but if a pin inspires you then you can contribute something to the conversation. You should make at least one comment each day. Make the comments as short or as long as you want. But you should ensure that your comment is not self-promotional.

5. Create Your Own Images

Create your own images and pin them to your Pinterest boards. These could be images that can be used with stand-alone graphics or blog posts. It is recommended that you do this all in one sitting. This saves time in production and concept.

6. Generate Content Ideas Using Analytics

Ensure that you review Pinterest analytics at least once a week. Evaluate your click progress, impression and repin. This will help you know which images and boards are attracting more attention.

Power Up Your Pinterest Traffic: Now that you know how to use Pinterest to generate traffic to your website, let's take to the next level. If you want to get MORE traffic and see MORE sales coming from Pinterest, here are a few more tips to keep in mind... Pair Short Blog Posts with Great Photos You don't have to write a 500-word article for every blog post you create. Instead, write a really interesting paragraph of 50 - 100 words and pair it with a great photo.
You can also include links to some of your other posts at the end. Then "Pin It" and watch the magic happen. With just 10 minutes of work, you can get several hundred visitors almost instantly! The best part is that people coming to your website from Pinterest will automatically encounter a variety of links to other pages on your website where they can explore and learn more. This is presents a great opportunity to advertise other products and services by using banners and text links. You can also make additional revenue by including Google AdSense on your website. Another technique that works great for me is to offer a free report or eBook to get visitors from Pinterest to sign up for my mailing list. Then I

promote other affiliate products and CPA offers to them over time, which generates even more money for me. The possibilities are truly endless. For more ideas, simply click on other people's Pins to visit their website and study how they monetize their website.

Pin Your Affiliate Links: This is a really neat way to make money using Pinterest, but you should use it sparingly or you will definitely look like a spammer. Create a board to pin products you love and then pin an affiliate link to Amazon, eBay, Clickbank or other affiliate websites. When you paste in the affiliate link, choose an image from the page (such as a book cover or product image on Amazon) and then pin it.

USING PROMOTED PINS: Promoted Pins are an ad option you can use on Pinterest. They are very targeted and show up only to those Pinners who are looking for your content. Promoted Pins use the power of the Smart Feed search to reach your target audience. You can use Promoted Pins for brand recognition campaigns, but there are other ways you might use them for. You might choose to use them to boost your traffic, build your brand, increase store sales or grow your visibility. Promoted Pins are available to all businesses and work well no matter what your niche or industry. What's more, Promoted Pins work on the CPC (cost per click) method, so you only pay for those who click on your pin. But many other Pinners will also get the chance to see your brand, which will prime them for future clicking, reading, subscribing, or purchasing. It's typical for Pinners to search for something they are preparing to do or to purchase. There is an average of 175 billion people who visit Pinterest each month, and they know that approximately 75% of the pins they will see will be from brands. Additionally, when a Pinner saves your Promoted Pin to one of their boards, their followers also see it in their feeds. This little feature gives you more bang for your marketing buck, especially since pins can be found for years to come. You may end up making sales from a Promoted Pin long after you ran the ad. In fact, according to Pinterest, "Advertisers receive an average of 20% more (free) clicks in the month after launching a Promoted Pin campaign." Because Promoted Pins are keyword-based, it's vital that you optimize your campaign with the right keywords to get your pin in front of your targeted audience. Pinterest gives you 150 keywords for each Promoted Pin, so you can include an assortment of competitive keywords that will make your marketing highly successful. Pinterest has made it easy to set up Promoted Pin campaigns. You just chose the best pin for the goal, set your goals, determine your audience and set your CPC budget.

Weekly pin focus: There's no wrong day to pin, but several studies have been conducted to find out what days are most popular for which topics.

• Monday—Starting off a new week of good intentions makes fitness and health the most popular.
• Tuesday—Technology and gadgets rule the day.
• Wednesday—We all need inspiration around Hump Day, which is why inspirational quotes are trending then.
• Thursday—Everyone's getting ready for the weekend, so fashion is on everyone's mind.
• Friday—Getting through that last day of the work week can be tough, which must be why comedy, especially GIFs, are popular.
• Saturday—Dreams of getting away make vacation and travel the top pins.
• Sunday—Ah, the day of rest leads to searching for good food and craft ideas.

Another study showed that the absolute best day for pinning is Saturday since that's a day most people can begin to rest and relax.

Add your URL or Logo to your pin: You should always include your logo and site URL on all Pinterest images. The goal is to get your pins repined many times to reach more people with your brand. Since pins are so evergreen, you could lose a potential buyer or fan if they can't find where the content comes from months or years after you post it. Adding your website info on the image ensures they know where to go for more content or details about the product.

Create step-by-step tutorial images: Pinners love how-to tutorials. You can use these as a way to demonstrate how to use your products as an easy way to get Pinner's attention and hard-earned cash. Once they learn how your products work and can imagine themselves using them, you'll quickly turn a visitor into a buyer.

Advanced Techniques

The above is the basic approach that you should be taking to your Pinterest marketing and it explains how you're going to go about providing value on a regular basis and growing your audience.

But if you want to step up your game, then you should look at using some of the advanced tools that Pinterest offers. Compared to other social media sites, the number of tools and support that Pinterest offers specifically for businesses and marketers is really quite staggering, so it's crucial that you start taking full advantage of this.

If you already have a Pinterest account, then thankfully there is the option to 'Convert Now' which lets you change your current account into a business account. This is completely free and takes a matter of seconds, so it's worth doing. From here, you can then install a Pin It button easily to your page, you can get a 'Follow Me' button to add to your website too, or you can set up your analytics.

Using analytics is an incredibly good idea, because it will allow you to see which of your articles and images are being shared on Pinterest and being interacted with. This is a hugely useful tool for assessing which of your content is performing the best and that helps you to refine your approach. Maybe your memes are getting the most shares? Maybe shorter articles perform better? Looking at these metrics let you know. This is a very powerful feature that a lot of other social sites just can't come close to!

We discussed the use of 'rich article pins' earlier but in fact there are actually six types of rich pins. These include:

- App
- Movie
- Recipe
- Article
- Product
- Place

That means that you can provide additional information about your pin and set up your site so that when someone else shares your pin, the additional information will be there automatically. For marketers, one of the most interesting types of pin other than the rich article pin, is the product pin. A product pin essentially enables you to show availability for an item and to show the pricing in real time. If you don't have the 'Buy' button on your pin, this is the next best thing for making it easy for people to buy your products and to learn more about them.

Pinterest has some useful utility for influencer marketing, thanks to its own 'Pinterest Email' feature, which was introduced in May 2013. This tool allows you to send your contacts on Pinterest a personalized message that might recommend a specific pin, or which can be used to open up a dialogue.

What makes this useful is that it means you can now get in touch with other users that are performing well on the site. In turn, this then means you can invite them to work together or can suggest particular partnerships. This can be beneficial for both brands and if you gradually approach more and more highly influential users, you can progress up the ladder to increase your rich.

You can also use this to turn prospects into buyers – send someone who is engaging with your content a pin that you think they'll like, or that you think will solve an issue they're having, and it could turn into a sale for you, or at least a new subscriber or follower!

If you want to go one step further with your website/Pinterest integration, then you should look into adding widgets. You can get widgets for both your Pinterest page and for your boards specifically. Either of these can then be added to the sidebar of your website, which will make your profile much more tempting for people to follow. Not only will your visitors be able to see that you're on Pinterest but this way they'll also be able to see the type of content you're sharing and the kind of value you're offering. This is also a great way to ensure that your website stays looking active if you're busy and don't have time to add new blog posts for instance.

As we mentioned previously, Pinterest is the perfect platform for launching a competition. The visual nature of Pinterest creates a fun opportunity for people to send in their ideas for interior design, or novel uses for your products. Likewise, you can run contests where you award the most inspiring boards on the platform that solve a particular problem that you posit. Either way, this is a great way to get more people engaging with your brand which can in turn also lead to more of your pins getting shared throughout social networks. When running contests though, make sure that you adhere to the guidelines that Pinterest sets out for brands.

If you want to make your marketing strategy even more advanced, then you should look at the ways you can leverage other tools and software to streamline your workflow. As we'll see, utilizing the right apps and services can save you a lot of time and help you to get more work done more quickly.
Here are some of the best ones to consider using...
(IFTTT.com) IFTTT is an absolutely incredible tool that allows you to synchronize a large number of different apps and services that you use on the web. It works by letting you set up certain actions on social media, web apps or even WordPress to

work as 'triggers. These triggers can then cause an action on a range of other connected services.

The most basic example of this would be to have your WordPress page automatically share posts to Pinterest when you upload them. Make sure you're adding in the rich article's metatags, and then let IFTTT take care of the rest by adding the articles to the pages automatically. This can save you a lot of time but do remember that you don't want to make all your content automatically added – you also need to actively select some of your Pinterest content to make sure that you're providing value.

There are also a ton of other 'recipes' (as they're known on the site) that you can create through IFTTT to streamline your Pinterest posting. For instance, why not have your Instagram pictures automatically shared to Pinterest as well? Or how about the Instagram pictures that you like? Alternatively, you can go the other tact and make sure that your Twitter followers are notified each time you add new content to Pinterest. Now, each new pin you add is another opportunity for your followers to gravitate toward your Pinterest account and increase the number of followers you have there. You can sync this up with any of your social media accounts which will help to keep your profile looking busy!

There is a Pinterest Chrome plugin that can save you a huge amount of time on Pinterest yet again. What this allows you to do is to easily share any image you come across online (as long as you're using the Chrome browser) by just hovering your mouse over it. This is much faster than having to navigate to Pinterest each time you want to add a photo and then manually enter the URL and it basically means you're more likely to add more high-quality content as you find it to your account.

Pinterest also has great apps for Android and iOS – both of which make it even easier for you to manage your account and to add new photos or respond to comments. The great thing about the apps is that you can use them wherever you are, which will again save you time and which means you can promote your brand when it's convenient for you instead of having it eat into your other business activities. The other great thing about the app is that if you hit the 'plus' sign in the top left, you can quickly take photos that you can then add as pins. If you have a personal brand, or if you want to show off your company hard at work in the office, then this is a great tool! Other than this additional feature, using the Pinterest app is broadly similar to navigating the website, so you should find it very intuitive.

Your Pinterest Plan

Now you have all the pieces, it's time to put them together to form a plan that you can follow one step at a time in order to build your viewers and to gain mass influence.

Step 1: Build Your Brand

The first step is to build your brand. This means you need to make sure that you know 'who you are' as a business before you tackle Pinterest. This is something that should come before you begin on any social media site. You need to make sure you have a clear 'mission statement' that ties all your different products, blog posts and activities together. This should then be expressed through a logo which should bleed through into your web design. Make sure you have a website set up that has a design language consistent with the rest of your branding and then bring that same color scheme and logo to each of the social media sites you sign up with.

It's this consistency that will ultimately ensure that each interaction with a customer increases your brand visibility and helps to build your authority. This will also considerably help you to appear more professional as you maintain the same design sensibilities in everything you do, rather than appearing not to have any particular strategy. The mantra of most businesses when it comes to social media marketing is to 'be everywhere' and consistency is key with that. Make sure your Pinterest account is a business account and link it with your website using the code that Pinterest gives you.

Step 2: Link Your Accounts

Now you should do a little prep work to make sure that your work flow is going to be as smooth as possible and to help yourself more easily add new content to your Pinterest boards/share users between your accounts.

Make sure that you have a link to your Pinterest page right on your homepage then and even consider adding a widget in your sidebar so that your visitors can migrate to Pinterest from there. Likewise, ensure that you Tweet about your Pinterest page and that you share your Instagram images on Pinterest. You can use IFTTT to set up some of these relationships and that will save you a lot of time. You should also install the Instagram app on your mobile device and the Instagram plugin for Chrome – both of which will make it easier for you to keep adding new content.

Use Shareaholic meanwhile to add social sharing buttons to your website, thereby allowing other people to share your content. This is also a good time to set-up rich article pins with your website so that the pins that do get shared from your website will have titles and information under them.

Step 3: Provide Value

Now begins the most important part of your Pinterest marketing strategy: delivering value. Make sure that you are posting content to Pinterest regularly and that you have come up with some kind of 'angle' for your boards that will really appeal to your audience. You might focus on inspirational images, beautiful images, or tips and ideas. Either way, your board should fulfil some kind of purpose and be useful to your followers. It should be so valuable as to essentially stand as its own 'product' and attract viewers on its own merit. Only occasionally will you then link your images back to products you're selling, or try to get people to sign up to your mailing list etc. Make sure to carefully choose the tags you add to your pins so that people can find your images and write comments underneath to provide context. Good titles can also help a lot. If you're still unsure of what works, then spend some time looking at the boards we recommended to get ideas.

You should also make sure to keep posting great value content to your website that people can share through Pinterest. Use analytics to see which content is performing best and make sure that you feature attractive images that will grab attention and get people to pin and repin. You should also spend some time interacting with the community and building relationships: that means repining the content you find from other users, posting comments and sending messages to your followers. This will help you to build more of a relationship with those users.

Step 4: Monetize

Monetization is the step that should come last, but of course it's still very important. The best way to monetize your Pinterest account is to add your own products or to mention your services in the text below your posts. The great thing about selling products through Pinterest is that the new 'Buy Now' button will allow you to sell directly like an eCommerce store. Otherwise, use the 'Rich Product' pins and use these to keep your viewers updated regarding the items you have in stock, the price and where they can get hold of them.

More important than these direct sales though are just to build your audience and to gain their trust so that you can bring them to your website when they're looking for services and products like yours. This is when social media is its most effective, so don't get impatient and drive them away!

As some final advice, consider the following 'dos and don'ts' to guide you through...

DO Make sure that all your content is offering real value for your followers.
DO Add useful descriptions to anything you upload.
DO Pick the right tags!
DON'T Just try to sell products!
DO Set up useful 'automated' systems to save you time.
DON'T Rely on these though, or you'll end up with a lot of random content.
DO Think about how articles you write for your blog post will work on Pinterest.
DON'T Post irregularly and leave your account looking barren.
DON'T Just rely on repining – add your own unique content!
DO Upgrade to a business account.
DO Verify your website so that you can see analytics.
DO Include social sharing buttons on your content.
DON'T Think that Pinterest is less important than other social media sites!
And while we're at it, let's consider some cool ideas for things you can do with Pinterest, which will hopefully leave you with a bit of inspiration before you get started.

Designing Your Website or Logo

A great way to get to grips with Pinterest is to try using it yourself not as a marketer. When designing your website or logo, you can use a Pinterest board to collect images that you like the looks of and that you think should inspire the artistic direction you're going to go with. You'll find this really helps you to bring everything together into a cohesive design at the end and this understanding will prove useful when you're trying to appeal to other users with your own content.

Bodyweight Exercises

If you have a fitness blog, then using it to share bodyweight exercises is a great idea. This is the kind of thing that allows you to provide genuinely useful tips but through just a single image and some text!

Eye Candy

Some people love staring at pictures of beautiful holiday locations, other people love looking at stunning cars. Sometimes creating a board that's all about making us salivate is a great way to get fans – and as you're building up the desire factor, it will be great when it comes to selling!

Life Hacks

People love lifehacks and actually Pinterest is one of the big reasons for this! Try posting tips that you can convey in a single image. Life hacks can also be applied to pretty much any niche whether it's 'gardening' life hacks or tidying life hacks!

Motivation

Motivational posters are popular online and can apply to a range of different topics. Why not create a board that focusses on motivational images and text relating to your niche or industry?

Those are just a few ideas, but the possibilities are endless so dive in and start experimenting! Good luck and happy pinning!

GENERATING TRAFFIC TO YOUR WEBSITE

The World Wide Web has truly pervaded all aspects of human existence. Everything and everyone are going online now, and the move towards a totally connected world is not "if" anymore, it's "when".

Statistics show that up to 85% of the people who spend time online also purchase online. If you take the North American continent alone where more than 75% of the population have an Internet connection at home, even if a fraction of these people buy online, it is still a huge market. Online purchasing is also seeing tremendous growth and many companies are projecting a doubling of volume in just three years. If you take PayPal as a case in point, they have gone from $2 billion in payment volumes in 2002 to $16 billion in 2009 with revenues crossing $2.4 billion.

Online is where you will have to be in the future and whether you are selling something or just blogging about your thoughts, if you are serious about it you will have to do something to increase web traffic to your site.

There are a number of ways in which you can do this and there are a number of people who give free advice on what you need to do to increase web traffic. One of the most common things you hear is SEO or Search Engine Optimization, and while this is something that you have to keep in mind, there are a number of other things that you can also think about.

The content that you put up on your website is the most critical thing that you need to think of. In the same way that a store will do well only if they sell things that people need, you will get people visiting your website only if you give something that people are looking for. Of course, it also means that you are entering a crowded market because genuinely unique niches are hard to come by. If you do find one, you are on to a good thing, but even if not, as long as you make the content appealing, you are sure to find takers.

Do something that others don't do. For example, selling products or services online is catching on really fast, and you will find a number of sites with products that link back to the larger online retailers like Amazon or eBay. If you want to do the same, it is not that difficult, except that there is something that you will have to give that other websites do not offer. For example, if you offer a personal review of the product that you are selling you are sure to develop a certain number of loyal customers and as long as the reviews are informative and helpful you will only get more customers with time.

There are other websites that offer the same thing, but most of them will have only a couple of lines that they probably found in other websites and copied. If you give information that is more detailed and specific, things that only a user would know, you are sure to make a hit.

Keep people coming back for more!

This does take more work and time, but unless you are willing to invest in good content, there is really no point in proceeding further. Make sure that you do your research. Even if you are only selling dog collars, as long as you give the pros and cons of each one honestly people will appreciate it. The goal should be to make the content such that people who even casually visit your site once will bookmark it and keep coming back.

Keep it short and simple

While writing your content, remember that just because you want to be informative you should not have long winded articles. Statistics show that between 400 and 600 words is the best length for most online articles. If you want to fill space in your site use other interactive content. Not only will this make the whole thing nicer to see and read it will also relieve the monotony of just plain text.

Even if you do not have the expertise to create interactive content, just using bullet points and charts in-between text will break it up into smaller more easily read pieces.

Stay who you are

Lastly, while writing, never lose your human voice. While writing it is easy to lose the personal touch that you give when talking and instead go for a more professional voice. The only thing that this will serve to do is to make visitors feel unwanted.

This becomes more of a problem as you grow, because as you see more money come in you will start to streamline the content. You need to walk a tight rope here because it is very easy to lose what brought people to your site in the first place while doing this. The risk of changing anything is that just as there is potential for success, there is an equally good chance for failure too.

One more thing that you should keep in mind when developing web content is that the more graphics you have, the more time it takes to load the page.

Give value

One of the best ways of generating interest in posts is to give insider information. Don't just write rehashed information that is easily found in other places online. If you are recommending a particular software for a specific purpose give honest impressions that are not found elsewhere. You may think that this is too much to give away freely but look at it this way. Open Source is catching on like blazes now, and there is a free alternative to almost everything, including Operating Systems. If you want to charge for your opinions as well as for the product that you sell, you will find that someone else is only charging for the product and is offering their opinions freely resulting in a movement away from your site.

Become a Community Member

If you are starting a website or blog, chances are that there is already an online community on the niche that you want to start yours in. Make sure that you become involved and join them. Don't get so high and mighty that you think that everything that you write online should get you money. Write on other people's blogs and websites too. Just make sure that you link back to your site. Usually this is done in the signature and is one of the most effective ways of generating traffic to your site as long as what you write is worth reading. If the posting was good, people will come to your site just to read other articles written by you which is what you want.

Quote, but link

Another way is to quote from an article written elsewhere on the net. Usually nobody minds you quoting as long as you give them credit for it and link back to their site as well. Not only is this good etiquette, it will also improve your standing within the community which means that slowly, other more established people will start to link to your site.

Apart from the traffic that this linking generates, there is another more valuable reason for doing this. Most search engines do not index a website as soon as it is hosted. There are a number of people who create sites on free to use communities and then do not follow it up. Obviously, no search engine wants any site like this in their results. One way that they identify if a site is in use and is genuine is by the number of links back to it. If these links are from sites in good standing with the search engines, the chances of your site getting indexer faster are greater.

Use article directories

Another very popular way of getting these links back is by posting articles on article directories and then linking it to your site. There are many such article directories that allow you to upload content free although they have certain criteria about the kind of articles that you can upload. Ezine is only one among them and there are a number of others that you can post to. What this does is help you upload a lot of content in places other than your website and then back link to your website thus improving your standing with the search engines. This is where you use the SEO optimization that you hear about frequently. There are two goals to doing this, one is the already mentioned improving of ranking with search engines, and the other is that sometimes these articles will actually come up higher in the ranking than your site. If this happens you will be driving traffic to your site from there too.

Use of Keyword Tools

This is one of the most important things that you will have to do. First, you will have to decide what the keywords are that most people may use when they want to look for what you are providing. Think about the words people would use to find your site, and the more people who contribute, the more exhaustive the list is going to be. After you have narrowed down the general keywords that you think that people will be looking for, you can use specific software like Google's keyword tool, Yahoo's Overture Keyword selector tool, Wordtracker, Keyword Dictionary or any other tool that you are comfortable with.

Most of them are free to use and will give you a combination of keywords based on the keyword that you typed in. This will help you identify the best combination of keywords to use in your content because it will give you the search strings that are the most commonly used in relation to the word you typed in.

Don't overdo it

This may sound simple but in reality, it is not. This is because you will have to walk a fine line between over-stuffing your articles with different keywords and with putting in too few. And even then, most search engines are able to identify if the keywords come logically as part of the sentence or have been forced in somewhere where they are not suitable. Nobody knows exactly how the search engines do this as it is their trade secret but suffice it to say that just because your article is full of keywords it does not necessarily mean that the site is going to get a better ranking. Often an article with the keyword appearing just once will pop up higher than one where it has been repeated a number of times. Keep this in mind when writing your articles. Also, never copy content, unless you are linking back to where you are copying from. All search engines are able to identify copied content and if it finds that your article is copied, you will even lose ranking because it will tend to push your site to the bottom of the pile.

Do your groundwork

This is not as easy as you would think though. You will first have to locate all the sites that are the leaders in the segment you are in. There are a number of tools that will help you do this, and Google PageRank is both very useful as well as free. After you form your list you will have to visit each of these sites and figure out for yourself why they are doing better than you. Check different search engines that will give you this information and this is where your true talent lies. The more accurate you are in identifying why others do well, the better you can make your site. While making changes you will obviously have to continue tracking hits to your site, but do not be hasty and make changes quickly. It will take a day for the changes to be indexed properly in the search engines, and even then, you will have to allow some time before the changes start making any difference. It is a slow process and you learn as you go.

Give Freebies

This does not mean that you give out free products. It could very well be a simple eBook on a particular subject or free wallpaper.
For example, if you have a website that is related to IT you could give wallpapers or screen savers that you have designed. Many people do this, but they ask for contact information as well. This is really a waste because the only reason for this contact information is to send out newsletters and as we have already seen, newsletters are really not all that effective. By giving it free without anything in return, you will be generating more interest in your site. Interest will spread by word of mouth and you will find people visiting you simply to download what you have to offer.

If you are opening a medical related site, giving out a short 10- or 20-page eBook on some ailment, say diabetes, will only do good. Of course, if this book is not a good one you will be better off not offering it for free as the reputation that you will receive will be bad. If you give out an informative well written book, or a really nice-looking wallpaper, people will talk about your site and ultimately the amount of publicity generated will be greater than if you had spent 10 times as much as you did for what you gave away.

Advertise!

This will of course cost money, but you have no other way around it. Any startup company needs marketing and even if it is online you will still have to market your wares. There are a number of innovative ways of doing this starting from fliers posted at different places to you having your website displayed prominently on your vehicle. Depending on the route you take the budget may be high or low and have varying degrees of effectiveness.

Go with AdSense

Not only offline but you can also go for online advertising. There are many websites that offer space to advertisers for a sum and you can advertise where you think you will get the maximum benefit. Pop ups, banners and advertisements are all popular, but the most popular is AdSense by Google. Anyone can sign up with AdSense and Google determines the kind of advertisements that go into the web-page.

If you want to advertise on other websites, you must place a sealed bid for the space and if you are selected you can advertise. If you want to sell ad space, Google takes care of everything but takes a 32% cut in the income generated. Even with this revenue loss it still makes sense to go with AdSense because a number of small operators who do not have the financial clout to do much have generated income from AdSense.

If you are purchasing ads, then the only thing that you are limited by is the budget you have. The more you have, the more you can advertise.

If you are looking at generating income through advertisements, you have to be a little careful about it. When your website is still new, and is not generating much traffic, many people will purchase ad space very cheap and then reap the benefit of all your hard work because they will be getting much more than what they paid for. It is better to wait a while until you get established before you start selling advertisements because of this.

Don't get too greedy

Another bad thing and more important when it comes to generating traffic to the website is that a site that is covered with ads just turns people off. You may start to earn money quickly by adopting this strategy, but many browsers do not like sites that have a lot of advertisements meaning that you will actually be losing traffic by advertising, although this is one income stream that you cannot afford to ignore.

How you balance your need for income generation with your website is where your talent lies, and how well you do depend on how right you get it. There is really no simple rule that you can follow here. There are a number of sites that are loaded with ads and yet do well, while there are others that do not have too many and still do not do as well. There are a number of factors that are responsible, and only time will tell whether you are right in what you did or not.

When you are developing your website, you need to have a vision of what you want from it. You are building up an organization, not just a website and the growth potential is limited only by your imagination. You need to establish a brand and live up to it. Of course, this takes time, but it is time well spent. You have to set expectations and make sure that you live up to them. If you are in the practice of putting in two posts a day, you will have to ensure that you continue to do so every day. You may complain that this means that you do not have any holidays or time off, and you will be right here. Yet, it will be worth it in the long run. Statistics show that even if you miss one day the traffic falls immediately. Of course, if you are going to miss only one day this is not a long-term impact, but if you are going to make a practice of doing this, you will start losing traffic instead of gaining it.

Plan ahead

If you feel that you absolutely have to take a break, make sure that you plan in advance for it. There are a number of things you can do starting from outsourcing this blog posting to making sure that you have a ready supply of posts that you can post from anywhere. The whole world is connected these days and as long as you have already prepared the articles, all it is going to take is 10 or 15 minutes of your time to post it every day.

If you are putting in articles regularly, make sure that the quality of your work does not flag. With success don't become complacent. Outsource some of the more labor-intensive work but make sure you check it for originality and quality. By staying on top of the work you choose to outsource your site will not lose the high standard that you want for your business.

Over time a certain website will stand for something, and you need to identify what this something is even before you start. Only then can you work towards it. If you just start without having any other goal than just that you want to earn money, there will be no direction to your site and it will vacillate here and there, never a good thing.

Optimize Content

This is a very important factor when it comes to developing your website. Optimizing the content does not only refer to SEO or search engine optimization, but also to the layout of the website as well as each page.

SEO

This is an acronym that has been used and reused so many times that many people think that this is the only thing about a website that makes it get a higher ranking. Obviously search engines will make use of keywords to index your articles, but the problem is that when writing content, we can only take into account a few words or phrases that we think is what the whole world is looking for. Yet, all search engines will pull out your articles even using other keywords, words that you would not consider as keywords at all.

The best thing to do is to use industry specific words to ensure that you have a wide distribution of words. For example, if you are creating a food website where you plan on putting up different recipes, make sure that you include all the words that you think will be used to search for your article. Words like cooking, recipes, dish etc. are all different words that can be used because it is all different ways for the public to search for the same thing.

There is fierce competition with regards to optimizing the content and most of the larger websites would make sure that they corral most if not all the keywords that they think are important. Yet, this does not mean that your site will be low down in the ranking. Ranking of a site by a search engine is based on a combination of factors and SEO is only one of them.

Layout optimization

Most search engines use programs called spiders or crawlers to index your site. These spiders or crawlers are nothing but programs that mimic human behavior but with the added capacity to tag and index everything that they visit. Generally speaking these crawlers go top to down and left to right. This means that the top left-hand corner of your site is the most valuable piece of real estate while the bottom right hand corner is the least.

Knowing this will help you to optimize your layout better. For example, if you are designing your home page, it would be a better idea to put in the links to other informational content on top and less important information like the about us link at the bottom.

Always tag pictures

Another thing that you should remember is that crawlers cannot read through graphics or scripts. This means that even if you subscribe to the belief that a picture is worth a thousand words, it is still a good idea for you to write a dozen words under the picture defining what it is. Only this text will be used by the search engine for its indexing purposes, which is why if you look up any result in Google images you will sometimes find that the images do not have anything to do with your search string, but the keywords would be present in its description.

Some people use this defect to leverage their site by adding in keywords that are not entirely suitable, and you are the only judge as to whether this is a risk worth taking. Search engines are always evolving, and if at some point in the future they redefine their algorithm so that they can identify such keyword stuffing, you will find that your website has all of a sudden lost its ranking. Google is definitely not going to notify the world that it is going to do this giving you time to change your site. When you find out it is already too late.

Meta-tags

If you had done a little bit of looking around before you started working on developing your website, you would have come across the term Meta tags. Many websites recommend that you use them when you develop your website. These Meta tags are nothing but HTML tags that are not visible on the page itself and are usually included inside the <HEAD> tag of the page.

Most of the advice will be towards you stuffing all your keywords within these tags. You can even put in keywords that do not occur within the body of the article itself. For example, if you are setting up a cooking website and plan on introducing various recipes and if one of the recipes have to do with making chicken dumplings, you can add this plus combinations of the same keyword like for example, good chicken dumplings, or best chicken dumplings or any other search string that you feel you want to add, but which may not necessarily sit well within the body of the article.

They don't work for keyword stuffing

Unfortunately, most search engines just ignore this tag and anything within. They started doing this nearly a decade back and nowadays even the use of this tag is highly debated in certain circles. The reason for this is because many web-masters started stuffing in keywords that did not have anything to do with their sites at all just to start directing more traffic there.

Anyway, the bottom line is that if you use this tag to stuff in keywords you may even be doing yourself harm because some search engines actually penalize sites that do this.

Where do I use Meta Tags?

This does not mean that Meta tags are totally useless. Some search engines use what is inside the Meta tags coupled with what is within the articles to get a better idea of what the site contains. This is why the initial advice was to only include keywords that are related to what you are writing about.

Another thing that you can do is to put in a short description of what the site is about within this tag. If we take the same cooking website as an example, you could write a short one-liner like this "A simple recipe to make chicken dumplings within 30 minutes". Usually this line would be incorporated to some extent in the summary that is given below your website in the search results page. This does not mean that all search engines will start to display what is within these tags, but you at least have some amount of control over what is said about your site. Even Google that has come out a few years back and said that they ignore Meta tags, nowadays incorporate at least some amount of what is available in the Meta tags in their summary.

Other uses

There are also other uses for Meta tags like if you do not want to index certain pages in your site, or if you do not want the search engines crawlers not to follow certain links in your site. Using Meta tags with the no index or no follow options will give you this. You may wonder why anyone would even want to not index their site, but there are cases when it is helpful. For example, if you have written an article on a certain subject, but over a few years you find that things have progressed and that this article may not be relevant any more, you have the option of removing that page, or archiving it. Unless you specify that you do not want this page indexed it will continue to show up on searches, and because it has been around far longer than the updated page will be higher in the rankings. You can also use the tags to specify the content type, like if it is text or graphics, and the language used. Although this does not make that big a difference, it is really helpful, especially for those sites that offer a number of language options. The search engines will be better able to index each page separately, instead of taking everything to be duplicate content.

Blog

Blogging is something that most web surfers do. They either have their own blogs or they comment on others'. Having a blog page where you can post your thoughts and have others respond is therefore a good idea. A blog is not a comments page for your article. A blog is where people can share their thoughts and that's it.

You can therefore have a website where you give reviews and sell software and have a blog where you can discuss everything from how a certain IT company is following trade practices to the state of the economy. These comments may not find suitable space anywhere other than your blog and having a separate page for it is a good idea.

Have your blog in your website

This is something that a number of people fail to do. They will have a website and have a blog, but they will both be in different domains. Some people actually go to the time and the effort of creating their own website but host their blogs using free software like WordPress. Leaving aside the impracticality of this, you will also be losing out on driving traffic to your site from your blog. Web traffic is not all generated through just one source and it is only by combining a number of sources that you get where you want to be. Blogs are one of these options. If you have started blogging about an interesting topic there is every reason for people to follow through to your website if it were in the same domain. By splitting them up in different locations you are losing on a certain amount of the traffic.

The best way is to host your blog as a sub-domain of your primary domain which is your website, and the worst is to use other hosting sites like BlogSpot or

WordPress. Of course, if you have your blog in your site you will have to purchase more server space, but then the charges are quite low.

Conclusion

Increasing traffic to your website is not an easy thing because there is no one thing that accounts for most of the traffic. If there were two factors that accounted for 50% of your traffic it is very easy to keep a track of it and ensure that there are no mistakes. Unfortunately, traffic depends on a lot of small things that together give you the numbers.

If you think SEO optimization is what you need to be doing to get higher numbers, you will be surprised to find that it is actually backfiring if you leave out on quality of the content. If you concentrate a lot on the layout and do not spend much time thinking about the browsing experience, you are once again not doing everything. It is like a jigsaw that has a number of small pieces that have to mesh together, and even if one is missing there will be a very noticeable hole in the picture.

The basics like the content, tagging, linking, and layout are the first thing that you need to think of, but this will only let you achieve a certain amount of the potential that your site is capable of. You will still have to market it properly which is where the "driving traffic" comes in. Because everything is so cheap on the net when compared to traditional marketing, your costs may be lower, but this is offset by the amount of competition that you will have.

I have tried to give you a general idea of all the things that you will have to think of when you start your website. The net is a dynamic place and is constantly in flux. These tips are the basics that you need to get right while starting out. Once you have done all this you will have to figure out innovative methods of marketing your site to take it to the next level.

I wish you the best of luck in your venture.

100 Social Media Marketing Tips

Here are 100 of the most important concepts to grasp to make sure that your platforms work for you and your business. Just so we are clear here is my definition of Social Media. Social Media is any online platform where people can have conversations and create relationships with other people. Social Media Marketing is when you leverage those relationships to market your products and service.

1. Connection - The social networks are built around this concept, so it is very important you get this first for success. You begin by connecting with your friends, family, and people in your target market. Then you connect with their friends and family. Before you know it, just a few connections become many.

2. Conversation - One of the most important things to remember on the social networks is you cannot begin with the end (sales). It's like going to a cocktail party. Would you go to a party, meet someone new and right away launch into a sales presentation? Of course not. You would first get to know each other this is what social media allow you to do online. You begin with a conversation, and you learn what your new friend needs and how you can help them.

3. Create Relationships - As you have these conversations online, you begin to get to know each other. This leads to a better understanding of what your new friends need and what they love to do. You find out how you can help them. Like all great relationships, it should be less about you and more about them.

4. Content - The saying on the Social Networks is CONTENT is king! Your goal is to provide useful, relevant, free content to all your new friends, so they can get a feel for what you do and how you can help them. Don't worry about giving away too much because strangely, the more you give, the more you will get in return. It's a huge paradigm shift from the traditional marketing model, but it does work.

5. Community Building - Your community is your core group of like minder individuals. They more time you spend on the social networks the bigger that community will become. It starts out slow but as your community grows the faster you will grow your connections because you have access to an ever-growing pool of people. For example, if you start with ten friends and each of them have ten friends you then have access to 100 people. Once you become friends with those people, you then can connect with each of their ten friends, and it just goes on and on in a geometric progression. Now not every one of their friends will become your friends but the larger the pool of choices the more chance you have to grow the number of people you have relationships with.

6. Caring - As human beings we all hunger for other humans to connect with. It's just built into our DNA. Because our jobs and family commitments isolate us a lot of the time, it becomes harder and harder to find and create connections. Our online communities can help to fill that void. The most successful communities are the ones where people truly care about each other and try to help each other. When you give of yourself, you open yourself up to receive more in return, and this is where Social media shines! It is the perfect platform for giving to others.

7. Clients - Studies show that people prefer to do business with other people they know like and trust. Once you grasp all the previous concepts the next logical step is for your friends to do business with you. The cool part about this is you don't need to "sell" your products and services. Those people who need what you are selling come to you presold. Because of everything you have given them for free online

8. Find People Interested In Your Product or Service

Social Media Marketing is an excellent way to find people interested in your product or service. You can easily find discussions and join in the conversation. Keep an eye on the conversation, drop in when you see where you can add value, offer tips and resources, however, do yourself a favor, Be Social! If you wade into the conversation with constant "buy my stuff" you will be ignored.

9. Deliver Quality Content

You can create blog posts, share pictures of your products, ask questions, conduct surveys, and write articles, share teleseminars and webinars. There are 100's of ways to share quality content. However, in the beginning, it can be challenging to know just what to post. You can find information that others have posted and share it. Remember this content does not always have to be yours, but please do give credit where credit is due. Make sure you name who created the content, they deserve the credit.

10. Gather Their Information

You may be creating a list of followers on Twitter or a great group of friends on Facebook, remember that information belongs to Facebook and Twitter, it is not yours. They could shut down, or god forbid, block you. You must have a way of gathering the information of the people who are interested in your product or service. There are various services out there such as Infusion Soft, 1Automation Wiz or Mail Chimp that can enable you to collect the names and email addresses of the people who are interested in your product or service. These systems will also enable you to follow up and stay in touch consistently and easily People ask me "just how do I make money with social media?" That would be similar to asking "How do I make money with a yellow page's ad?" Social media is where you find people who are interested in your product or service and where people find you. Take the time to learn it yourself or find someone to do it for you.

11. Share tips, tricks, and ideas

If you have a way to help do something faster, share it with others. They will appreciate it.

12. Retweet or repost other people's stuff

This one will get some great Social media love going on, and they will be more likely to help promote you as well.

13. Be part of the conversation.

Don't just post your stuff. Talk to people, share with them. Offer advice and help them out. Comment on what they have going on as well.

14. Be consistent.

Don't slack off. Ideally, you will post once a day, but at least post once a week. Keep connected with other people. Reply to their comments, ask questions, and answer other people's questions. But post often. You can't expect to be good for a week and then let it go to nothing. People will think you dropped off the Earth and stopped following you. They will give up on you because they expected you to be part of the conversation and you let them down. It takes time and consistency to work for you.

Pretty much every marketing venue out there is the same, but social media marketing is more so than anything else I have ever seen. Let me tell you about an example of this. I have a lot of followers on Twitter. From time to time I like to go in and clean up my list. One of the first things I do is look for people that haven't posted for a while. I just wiped out over 100 people that haven't posted anything in over six months. YES, six months!

Many of these people started their accounts for business, and then were really good for a month or so and then gave up on it. They stopped posting and say that Twitter isn't a good marketing tool. Now I hear this about just about every type of marketing I see people trying from postcards to networking, to newspapers, to online marketing. Too many business people think that they can just try it for a bit and if it doesn't work, drop it and move to the next shiny object.

If you want any marketing to work, you have to give it time to work. People aren't going to buy from you right away. They don't know anything about you. They need to get to know you first and get to trust you. Especially, with Social Media. It's a harder place to get people just to buy. It's exactly what the name implies "Social" media. That means that you have to be social and build a relationship with your followers. And one of the most vital things is that consistency will help you build that relationship.

With all the tools out there to cross promote your social media sites like Twitter, Facebook, LinkedIn, etc., there isn't any reason you can't keep up with it. I spend about 15 minutes a day, and most of that is actually in direct communication with other people. By the way, that 15 minutes is for ALL of my social media sites, not just one.

You need to keep up with it. If you can spend 5 minutes to post something that you can share with your followers, it will build each and every day. You will build a better relationship with those people and the byproduct of that... more sales. Here is a couple of things that you can post that will help build that relationship with others.

By just following these few steps a few minutes a day you will build up a large following of loyal fans that want to know what you have going on and share out your message with their followers. But, be consistent. Don't let your work go to waste. It's going to take a bit longer, but you will have a much stronger following, and people will be much more likely to want to hear what you have to say.

14. Connection to a combative diary post: There's nothing higher for inspiring engagement than somewhat disputation.

16. Let Interest move you: Interest could be a goldmine regarding finding staggering pictures you'll share (especially pictures with quotes). Essentially make a point to offer right credit.

17. Share a valuable asset: If you're included concerning sharing the first accommodating information along with your adherents, don't be hesitant to direct them to various individuals' significant substance (not just your own).

18. Post a Slide Share Introduction: If you might want to search out one that is as of now turned out to be very much enjoyed, visit the 'Inclining in Social Media' segment at the most reduced of the Slide share landing page.

19. Connection to a contextual investigation: Case examines pleasant for conveying accommodating data in an exceedingly way that is extra food and vile than an average weblog post.

20. Connection to partner industry-related IFTTT formula: Haven't distinguished of IFTTT (short for If This Then That)? You might want to find out it out. At that point share a connection to a recipe your supporters would see accommodating.

21. Fire audits or tributes: Eliciting surveys from fans or devotees is one among the best ways that to encourage tributes you'll use as social verification on your site.

22. Fan photographs: scrounge around for hashtags related to your business or item, and offer a client picture on Facebook, Instagram or Pinterest.

23. Advocate an instrument: Share an (ideally free) device or asset you're suspecting that your supporters would notice helpful.

24. Share a most loved book: practically like #23, offer a book suggestion your fans or supporters would appreciate.

25. Every day inside the life post: gives a recap of a commonplace day inside the lifetime of a visual creator, creator, CEO, and so forth.

26. Advocate your most loved items: If you're AN internet business site, share a stock of your high merchants or most noteworthy evaluated item. In case you're an administration provider, share a stock of the item that helps you achieve your business.

27. Share irregular tips: sporadically post an arbitrary tip or trap your supporters would acknowledge accommodating. Imply: abuse irregular tip numbers add enthusiasm to your post (e.g. Tip #256: _____)

28. Connection to your most smoking web log post: gives a transient introduction to the post and put forth a defense for why it's your most sweep and shared post.

29. Offer a proposal: Share the affection by prescribing a business you've worked with accomplishment inside the past.

30. Share a work/life adjust tip: Your web-based social networking adherents wish to comprehend you're a genuine individual with proportional battles as them. Share a tip you've learned for an evening out work, life, and family.

32. Bring a visit to a world of fond memories: Share photographs of late logos, sites or your awfully starting item.

33. Arbitrary posts that show you're a genuine individual: for instance, what you had for supper the previous evening or what you're doing this end of the week.

34. Share boundless Reddit subject: Visit Reddit's Trending Subreddit page to search out across the board and slanting themes to post concerning.

35. Advocate another person to take after via web-based networking media: Share a connection to another person's webbased social networking profile and urge your fans to "like" or tail them.

36. Share a Pinterest board: If your clients are on Pinterest (imply: if your statistic is instructed, high-salary females, they more likely than not are), offer a Pinterest board using Facebook or Twitter.

37. Share a comic book or image: acquiring your clients to snicker with you might be a decent approach to begin building connections.

38. Post a video tribute: Share a video survey; or higher, be that as it may, raise your online networking devotees to present their video tributes.

39. Advocate a partner on LinkedIn: Encourage your associations with accomplishing never going to budge some person UN organization goes about as a profitable asset for your business.

40. Hold icon photograph} challenge: Fire photograph entries so get your fans to vote. Share the triumphant photographs, as well!

41. Share an inclining Twitter theme: Use Topsy to search out a substance that is far reaching and slanting on Twitter.

42. Have a dialog via web-based networking media: this could increase before long, subsequently, make sure to stay on high of it!

43. 'Inscription this': Post a photo and raise your fans to return up with imaginative or entertaining subtitles.

44. YouTube video see an adorable or consecrated video and induce you to purchase to your fans or supporters.

45. Tag another Facebook page: Generate some sensible fate by serving to push another business.

46. Share breaking the business news: be a stop of what's occurring in your business or specialty by exploitation Google Alerts.

47. Share nation particular occasions: need your supporters from round the world Merry Christmas (a full rundown of overall occasions is frequently found

48. Offer (and raise for) forecasts: for instance, "I anticipate that Germany can win the planet Cup. Who does one accept can win?"

49. Supply a free digital book: Build your email list while producing some goodwill alongside your fans.

50. Bring up issues: Let your fans raise you something.

51. Post a question see: Play argumentative third party, however, tread critically.

52. Utilize Facebook Interest records for substance thoughts: See what points square measure drifting and offer them alongside your fans or utilize them to think of your substance.

53. Profile a worker: Let your adherents comprehend they're adapting to genuine people.

54. Post item review sees: Keep your ear to the base in this manner you'll have the capacity to be the essential to share fundamental wellbeing information alongside your adherents.

55. Post a 'truth or fiction' address: Let your fans figure regardless of whether it's the truth or a story.

56. Share an inclining Google seek: Visit Google's high Charts to seek out what people square measure is presently searching for; give your particular turn on one in every one of these subjects.

57. Enthusiast of the Month: Acknowledge your total ministers and enable them to comprehend they're valued.

58. Share exchange investigation: Post a connection to and synopsis of research your fans would see accommodating.

59. Hold a blazing deal: Use Snap chat to supply a constrained time coupon.

60. Celebrate odd occasions: For example, did you know June 17 is Apple Strudel Day? Utilize an apparatus like Days of the Year to discover what today's vacation is.

61. Honors or awards you've gotten: Just do this painstakingly... the thought is to fabricate trust, not to boast.

62. Advance another person's deal: Share a connection to a coupon or deal from a complimentary (not contending) business.

63. Most recent organization news: Anything changing in your business? New representative? New hours of operation? New item advertising?

Share pictures from a current industry occasion: Don't neglect to utilize the occasion hashtag for a greatest introduction.

65. Advance a free download: This could be a module, white paper, digital book or whatever else that would be helpful for your gathering of people.

66. Thank your fans: A basic thank you can go far too building associations with your fans.

67. Offer master experiences into a point: This sets up you as an idea pioneer in your field.

68. Do a post arrangement: We do this on our web journals, why not via web-based networking media? Share a progression of comparable posts over a specific number of days.

69. Week by week round up: Post a rundown of the 'must read' articles for the week.

70. Get your workers to visitor post: Have your representative's alternate posting a 'fun reality' on Facebook or Twitter.

71. Make and offer an aggregation of industry news stories: Flip board is an awesome approach.

72. Have a Google+ joint: Promote it through all your online networking channels.

73. Urge your devotees to bolster a cause: Post a connection to an online pledge drive (and add to it yourself).

74. Post a specialist cite: Ask an industry expert a question and post their answer via web-based networking media. This is incredible for getting retweets and offers.

75. Hold a giveaway: This can be as straightforward as asking your fans or adherents to remark to enter.

76. Offer a sneak look: Whet your fans' hunger by demonstrating a sneak look at an up and coming blog entry, challenge or item dispatch.

77. Begin a discussion with an industry pioneer: Tag or say an industry master in a post (simply know you may be left hanging!).

78. Post a photograph montage: A device like PicMonkey can help you make one.

79. Secret substance: Posting a connection to a blog entry? Try not to uncover the punch line. This will, as a rule, increment your clickthrough's.

Make an industry forecast: Speculate on what's in store for your specialty or industry.

81. Post an innovative or surprising use for your item: Be certain to likewise approach your fans for thoughts.

82. Connection to a blog remark: Have an especially accommodating or dubious remark on your blog? Post a connection and get your fans and supporters to say something.

83. Answer a FAQ: Have a question you get asked a great deal? Answer it via web-based networking media.

84. Present a connection on old pamphlets: Recycle your bulletins and increase new endorsers in the meantime.

85. Approach your fans for substance thoughts: Find out which issues or issues your fans require help with.

86. Present a connection on an accommodating Facebook or LinkedIn gathering: If you are aware of a supportive asset on Facebook or LinkedIn, share a connection with your fans.

87. Recount a story: Share an entertaining or intriguing account from your life.

88. Discover what your rivals are sharing and improve: A simple approach to do this is by utilizing an apparatus like Social Crawlytics.

89. Utilize your site examination to discover content Thoughts: Take a speedy look through your investigation to discover which points produce the most enthusiasm from your group of onlookers.

90. Add in exclusive offers mostly to people who follow you on social media accounts. Grab your customers with a unique post. You can also include a contest for all the fans on your social media site. If contests are not your thing, you can still give your followers access to deals that regular customers won't be able to get.

91. Share a supposition: Your devotees need to know you remain for something; don't be reluctant to take sides on an issue (the length of you can and do remain behind your perspectives).

92. Present a connection on a representative Bio: If you have profiles on your site, present a connection on help your fans become acquainted with the brains behind your organization.

93. Answer a question from Quora: Find an important question on Quora and answer it via web-based networking media.

94. React to a tag or say: See who's been attempting to stand out enough to be noticed and react to them in a post.

95. Post an extract from a blog entry: Rather than simply posting a connection and rundown of the post, cut and glue an especially fascinating selection to arouse your per users' advantage.

96. Share an outline: Share an intriguing diagram or chart that is important to your group of onlookers.

97. Post a screenshot of an online networking discussion (with consent): Add your contemplations to the discussion.

98. Advance an industry-related occasion: This can either be a live or online occasion.

99. Share an amusing business: Post a business that would claim to your fans or supporters.

100. Advance your items or administrations: There's a reason this one keeps going on the rundown. There are a period and a place for self-advancement via web-based networking media, however as a matter of first importance, utilize online networking to assemble connections, set up trust, and construct your notoriety for being an industry master. At the point when individuals would like to purchase, who do you think they'll come to first?

Be aware of what time of day you get more responses and retweets on your Twitter page. Find out when your followers are online and post your updates at that time. Regardless of how it fits into your schedule, you want to send your tweets when the largest number of followers are likely to see them. An automated service can help you launch your messages in this ideal window.

You want to eliminate any overlap between your professional and personal Facebook presence. You probably don't want your followers to know too much about your personal life. If using your real name on a professional Facebook profile, try using a nickname on the personal page to prevent being found via a search.

Use pictures to effectively market your brand on social media websites. Pictures can often speak louder than words. They can help consumers to visualize brands and become interested in purchasing yours. Include pictures of your products, pictures of events you have attended, and any other interesting pictures that are worth talking about.

You should do your homework and find out what works best with social media marketing. Tools and options differ between sites.

If you don't already have a Yahoo account, make one, so you can go through Yahoo Answers. This portion of the Yahoo website is a service that allows people to submit questions, which other users then answer. Look up questions about issues related to your products, and write an answer mentioning your products.

Social media has actually existed for quite some time, even though it may not seem like it. Social media is so popular at the moment that a business absolutely must utilize it to succeed. Since social media is still in its infancy, it will continue to evolve for some time to come, but the basics should stay constant. Social media is growing off late at a faster pace than ever before, a properly planned and effectively targeted social media marketing campaign can help your small business thrive and succeed.

Whichever sites you pick, make sure to add quality content that you enjoy. Spamming is ugly no matter what type of marketing it is being done in. People want value, so give it to them. Also, be diligent in picking the tools you use to automate. Look for quality features and a great reputation when you choose your tools for success. These tips will help you to build up your business using social media. The websites you're personally using each day could be effective and helpful for business use. You can reach a global audience with social media and thrive thanks to tips from this book.

Conclusion

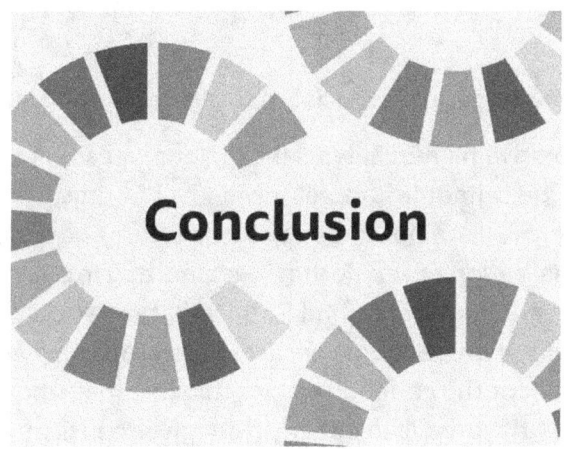

Conclusion

If you are looking to promote your online business on the internet, you have your work cut out for you. You really do. The difficulty does not come from finding traffic options. In fact, the difficulty comes from the fact that there are just simply too many options out there. It is too easy to get caught up in all the available traffic generation options, and spend a lot of time, effort and money only to have very little to show for all your marketing efforts. If you are serious about driving highly targeted traffic to your website, one of the best moves you can ever make is to carry out a forum marketing campaign. It is easy to understand why forum marketing works. Regardless of how obscure your niche is, there are already people congregating online at certain websites who are talking about different aspects of whatever it is you are promoting. They are congregating at online message boards also known as forums.

This is a tremendous marketing opportunity because it is like fishing by shooting fish in a barrel. The fishes are already in the barrel. They have already selected themselves and they are in a tight space. It is almost a sure deal. It is very hard to miss. However, you have to do this properly; otherwise, your forum marketing efforts will fail. Just as it is very easy to see the opportunities apparent in forum marketing, it is also very easy to completely blow those opportunities.

Here are the 10 secrets to forum marketing that can take your online business to the next level.

Secret #1: Niche targeting is crucial to forum marketing success

If you want to drive high-quality traffic to your website, you have to understand that you cannot just target any and all forums. That is a sure recipe for disaster. Why? You are not targeting these forums based on interest. Every forum has a specialization. Every forum is geared towards certain subject matter categories. It is very important to find forums that are specialized in the particular niche of the product or service you are promoting and stick to those forums. Do not fall for the common trap of thinking that since there are few forums that deal with your niche directly, you have to pick any and every forum. That is completely wrong. You are only setting yourself up for your failure if you think that way.

Secret #2: All your forum traffic must have an archive-able HOME

It really would be a shame if you put in all this time, effort and energy driving traffic from forums to your target website only to have that traffic evaporate. Unfortunately, that is precisely what you are doing if you are just promoting a link. Many old school marketers used to do this, and it used to work fine. Unfortunately, as forum visitors have become more sophisticated over the years, the old tricks simply are not going to fly. People expect more. People are not simply going to convert right off a link. I do not care how well written your landing page is. I do not care how well put together your sales page is. People expect more. Moreover, for you to maximize the traffic benefits of your target website, you need to make sure that it is archivable. It means that the content on your website must be arranged and handled in such a way that search engines can send traffic to different parts of your website. This is why I highly recommend that you create a blog. Many people think that a blog is a waste of time or it would take too much effort, but the reality is that thanks to outsourcing, it has become very easy to keep a professional blog. You want that traffic to go to specific pages on your blog, and you want other specific pages on your blog to work to convert whatever traffic you drive to your blog. You have to remember that different people have different interests. They have different reasons for clicking on a link to go to your blog. Your blog has to present the value proposition you bring to the table in many different ways, so as to maximize the commercial appeal of whatever it is you are promoting.

Secret #3: Forum link dropping campaigns WILL blow up in your face

One of the most commonly used forum marketing methods is to take simple links and just drop them in posts in forums. The problem with this way of marketing is that there is really no added value as far as forum readers are concerned. They do not have a clear idea as to the context of the link and how that link will add value to their lives. All they see are some catchy text encouraging them to click on the link. They do not even know in advance whether the link will be directly relevant to the niche of the content that they are interested in. Not surprisingly, many marketers that engage in simple link dropping campaigns have very little to show for all their efforts. In fact, most of them have nothing to show for their efforts because these forums end up banning them. That is right. If your account gets banned, all your posts get deleted. This is a serious problem because many forums marketers' market by simply dropping a link in either the body of their post or in their signature line. Regardless of whether you are using forum post body text or signature lines to promote your affiliate product or your own website, if you get banned, you will get to no benefits. This is why it is really important to understand that while you are, at the end of the day, promoting a link, you should not just promote the link. You have to promote content. You have to provide some sort of context for your link. At the very least, this would give people enough information, so they can make an informed decision as to whether the link will add value to their lives. If you are just dropping mysterious links all over the place, you probably will not get too many clicks since people are very scared of landing on Spyware injection or virus propagation sites. At worst, you will get banned. If you keep up this behavior, chances are quite high that your account will completely disappear from the forums that you are marketing at.

Secret #4: Credibility is the name of the forum marketing game

In secret #3, I have outlined the importance of content. Content is crucial because you cannot just drop naked links all over the place. People would not know what to do with your link. They would be very suspicious. They would be very skeptical and would often end up wasting all your time, effort and energy just dropping those links. Also, forum posts that only contain naked links look awkward. They look incomplete. At the very least, they look suspicious. This is why it is extremely important to clothe your links with credible content. Not only do you have to provide context for your link by including content, the content has to be credible. Credibility really can be boiled down to giving people reasons to trust you. That is the bottom line. People will only listen to you if they feel that you know what you are talking about. Unfortunately, too many forum marketers are completely ignorant about this forum marketing secret. They are very happy with simply dropping links. It is no surprise then that they enjoy very little success. If you want to really maximize the amount of benefits and value you can get from a forum marketing campaign, it is extremely important for you to focus on credibility. How do you build credibility? First, you have to offer real content. This is content that adds value to people's lives. This is content that actually answers specific questions that people have. Credibility arises from the usefulness of your participation in a forum. One thing is clear. Somebody who simply just drops links all over the place is a completely useless forum member. On the other hand, somebody who is always there to answer people's questions and steer them to the right direction will not only be viewed as a helpful person, but people are more like to click that person's links because they trust that person's information. I hope you see the difference. In fact, the difference is like day and night. If you are serious about making more money online through forum marketing, you need to start with a serious credibility building campaign.

Secret #5: Build faster credibility by piggybacking on competitor content

I know that the discussion on secret #4 may have gotten you worried. This is completely natural and perfectly understandable. If you think that building credibility will take quite a bit of time, effort and money, you are absolutely correct. If you are simply going to be posting completely original content and answering other forum member's questions directly on your own, expect to spend a lot of time and possibly quite a bit of money building credibility. Unfortunately, not everybody has that kind of capital. Not everybody has money set aside for a serious credibility building campaign on forums. Many online marketers are actually self-funded. In other words, they are using whatever meager income they generate from their online marketing efforts to bankroll their promotion efforts. If you are just starting out, then you are stuck in a classic chicken or egg dilemma. You do not have any money, but you need money to promote your website through a credibility building forum marketing campaign. The good news is that you can build credibility without spending money on original content. Best of all, you can build quite a bit of credibility quickly. The solution is actually quite simple. The solution, at least in the beginning, is to simply use your competitor's content. That is right – you piggyback on their best content. You might think that this is some form of plagiarism. You might even think that this is some form of theft. That is absolutely wrong. In fact, your competitors would love you for this because at the end of the day, you are driving traffic to them. Little do they know that their best content is actually benefitting you as well. When you answer questions in forums with the best content produced by your competitors, you build credibility. People can see that you are always ready with the very best useful content. This can only improve your stock as far as forum popularity is concerned. If you keep this up long enough, you can become quite an authority when it comes to certain subjects. That is where you need to go and the best way to do that is to simply piggyback on your competitor's best content.

How do you do this? You compile a decent list of all the top competitors in your niche who offer the very best content. When you see niche-related questions on forums, you can then do searches on your list of target blogs and websites to find the very best answer. You then post a link along with an explanation of as to why that link is a good resource. At the very least, the link answers the question being asked as well as providing other value. If you keep this up long enough, people will consider you the "go to" source for certain concerns. You can quickly become an authority in certain subjects.

By being quick to answer niche-specific questions that deal the subject area of the items you are promoting, you quickly become indispensable. Other experts might not be available. Other authorities may not respond to quickly. If you respond to niche-specific questions very promptly and you always supply really good answers, it is very easy for people to think that you are simply indispensable. The forum simply cannot continue to talk about certain subjects without you being in the mix. This is exactly the kind of perception you want to build. Unfortunately, it is not going to build itself. It is not going to happen on its own. You have to make it happen. The way to do this, of course, is to simply be there and be quick to respond to niche-specific questions. Try to be the first person to answer. Not only will you be able to build your credibility answering quickly, but the high placement of your answer ensures that you get more eyeballs. The more eyeballs you educate regarding your subject matter expertise, the easier it is for people to think you are indispensable. You need to keep this up until you become a solid authority.

The good news is that the timeline from zero to hero varies from forum to forum. Highly active forums take a longer time to be viewed as an authority at very busy forums because there is a lot more content being published. However, in slower forums, you can expect to become an authority quickly since you are one of the few people posting on a regular basis. The secret to all this, of course, is to keep it up. Do not expect things to happen overnight, just do this out of habit, just respond out of habit, and you will become an authority sooner rather than later.

Secret #6: Adopt a LARGER-THAN-LIFE persona

Most people want to post just like everyone else. Not surprisingly, they don't stand out. Their posts, no matter how awesome, simply fall between the cracks. There's no OOMPH power behind their posts. If you want your posts to truly stand out and GRAB and SLAP eyeballs, you need to put your personality on CENTER STAGE. In fact, you need to adopt a larger than life persona. You need to be SO LOUD, SO DEMANDING, SO COMPELLING, that you become UNAVOIDABLE.

Secret #7: Mix only your best content with your posts

The secret to forum marketing, of course, is to get people to click on your links. This is going to be a problem because as I have mentioned in secret #5, you are using other website's content to build your credibility. This is going to conflict with your overarching end goal of getting people to click only on your content. How do you make this happen? It is very simple. You mix your own content with the best agreed or high-quality content produced by your competitors. In the beginning, you are only offering competitor content. However, as your authority begins to build, you start mixing in more and more of your own posts and your own website links. It is really important that regardless of how much of your own materials you mix in with best agreed competitor content, that you exercise a high degree of discrimination as far as your content is concerned. Do not just mix in any of your post. That is not going to cut it. You have to zero in on your best content when mixing content sources. It is important to note that "best" is defined in this context as something extremely relevant. In other words, if somebody asks a question regarding toothpaste, you need to show your own blog's content that deals directly with toothpaste. I hope that much is clear.

Also, that content must pack enough information so that not only is the direct question answered sufficiently, but the blog post or article is rich enough that it answers other related questions ahead of time. That is how you can tell a high-quality piece of content with a shallow piece of content. A shallow piece of content will only answer direct question and nothing else. There is really not much added value there. A high-quality piece of content not only is deeper, but it also has the right graphics. If possible, it should even have video.

Secret #8: All your posts must lead to one place: AUTHORITY

As I mentioned earlier, you should mix your best content with your posts. However, regardless of what you do, all your posts must lead to you becoming an authority. If you are posting just for the fun of it, you are not doing it right. If you are posting just to get along, you are wasting your time. You have to be very careful as to what you post on a forum. You have to understand that authority is a very fragile thing. If people see you posting garbage, all that hard work, time and attention to detail that you put in previous posts go straight down the toilet.

You do not want that to happen. This is why you really need to be very careful regarding how you engage other forum members as well as the specific materials you post. If you abuse or make fun of other forum members, this kind of behavior can only undermine whatever authority you built up to that point. Always be aware that you are at a forum for a reason. Always treat other people respectfully. Always be serious about delivering solid value to the lives of the readers of that forum. This is the best way to build authority. It is all about consistency. It is all about sending clear message that builds up your credibility.

Secret #9: How to get other forum leaders to build your credibility

A forum is like an online neighborhood or an online city. In any city, there are influential people. These are people that other neighbors pay attention to. These are people who call the shots. There are two kinds of leaders. There are natural leaders and there are self-made leaders. Natural leaders simply ooze charisma. For some reason or the other, people are inexplicably drawn to these people. For some reason of another, other people give these individuals the benefit of the doubt. They simply attract people naturally. There are forum leaders that fall into this camp. For some reason, the way they post, the way they joke, and the way they carry themselves naturally draws others to them. They have a very strong personality that is very hard to resist. On the other hand, there are self-made leaders. This is probably where you come in. These are people who build their authority by their actions. It means that they really go out of their way to share certain types of content and engage with people a certain way, so people can trust them. These people are self-made. In other words, their actions made them.

Regardless of which type of forum leader you are interacting with, it is extremely important that you consistently work to get them to help you build your credibility. How do you go about doing that? It is very simple. By sharing high-quality content and then referring to them for their feedback or referring to their previous posts, you end up dragging them into your posts. This is not going to work all the time nor do not expect this to produce stellar results overnight. This is something that you do consistently over a long period of time. The more you mention these other forum leaders, the sooner you will get on their radar.

Once they start looking at you as some sort of ally or some sort of equal, do not be surprised when they start talking about issues that you raised before. Do not be surprised if they start sharing links that you shared in the past. This is what you want to happen because they lend you their credibility. They lend you whatever authority that they have built. If people in a forum think that they are people to be trusted, subconsciously those followers would start trusting you as well. Why? The people that they trust find you credible. In other words, these forum leaders vouch for you.

The best way to get them to lend you their credibility is to simply engage them with high-quality content. Always draw them in by mentioning them or referring to their previous posts. The key here is to be viewed as a peer. You cannot do this if you are simply just posting your own stuff over and over again. You are not giving existing opinion leaders and influential forum members a reason to lend you their credibility if you are just so focused on self-promotion.

Secret #10: Increase conversions through targeted forum posts

If you apply the first nine secrets of this list, chances are very high that you can drive quite a bit of traffic to your landing page or your squeeze page. That is all well and good, but the problem is all that traffic is not really going to benefit you all that much if you cannot convert that traffic into sales. The whole point of online marketing is to convert online traffic into dollars in your bank account. Unfortunately, if you turn a blind eye to conversions, you are simply rolling the dice with all that traffic. Nine times out of ten, that traffic is just simply going to bounce out of the landing page, squeeze page or blog post that you are directing that traffic to. In other words, you are simply wasting your time. You have to focus on conversion. In the beginning of your forum marketing campaign, you can be forgiven if you forget about conversions. The key focus at that point is to simply position you as an authority. At that point in time, your main goal is to build your credibility, so people can trust you enough to click your own content links once you start sharing your own content.

However, once you start sharing your own content, it is really important to make sure that the traffic that you are sending has a high chance of converting. One of the best ways to do this is to post selected content. In other words, you create highly specialized conversations that deal with topics that are directly relevant to your own content links. The key here is to get people excited about the subject matter that they read your forum posts. Open their minds to different possibilities and open their minds to wanting to know more. You then offer a link to your blog or website that gives them information regarding the topic that you raise in your discussion. The secret to all this is the know-like-trust buying process. When people click on your link, they are not yet ready to buy. They do not know enough to trust you. The key here is to give them more information. Get them to feel that they know you. You do this of course with your blog or website content. However, your content is engineered in such a way that people who feel they know you already can click a link, so they can compare whatever options you bring to the table with the other options available out there. These are people that are looking for reasons to like your solution.

Once you give them that content and they really like your solution, the next step is to link them out to your sales page. The sales page should then be written in such a way that it maximizes the trust people have in your solution. That is how it works. For anybody to buy anything from you, they must first trust you. However, for them to trust you, they must first like you. In turn, for them to like you, they must first feel that you know what you are talking about. These are all interrelated. You cannot just jump from the know stage all the way to the buy stage. It does not work that way. Keep this in mind, so that your blog or website content mirrors the know-like-trust process that is playing out when people read your targeted posts on forums.

Forum marketing can either be a hit or miss affair or it can be like shooting fish in a barrel. It all depends on how you carry yourself. Follow the 10 secrets outlined above to take your forum marketing results to the next level!

5 Ways To Never Run Out of Content To Share on Social Media

You've probably heard the joke, "So where do you want to hang out on our phones Friday night?" But, Yowwwzers!!! What did we ever do before smart phones and social media? So, you're hip to the content marketing trend. The question is how do you continue to find new and engaging content that will keep your readers running back to you instead of your competitors?

Here are some great places to look:

Reddit.com is a great place for social media revelation. Tens of millions of users hop on Reddit every day to discuss every kind of post and topic in the solar system. Have no fear of finding a mixed-up mess; it's all divided into sub-reddits where you can dive into your niche and get plenty of inspiration! The best part is, by checking the stats on a given topic, you can see how popular it is before running with it.

Feedly.com is a site that helps you focus your research. You can search journals, YouTube channels, blogs, and set up keyword alerts. You can also organize all of the sources that you choose, including content from your own website. You'll spend less time looking for what you need when you feed on Feedly!

Scoop.it is a site that is dedicated to social media content building. It offers content curation services and content marketing automation. Sign up for free, and you'll find a plethora of resources that 2.5 million bloggers and marketers already trust. Scoop.it allows you to embed content in your website, add your own thoughts to a post, share content on your social media, and search by keywords. It's a homerun hero in the blog and social media world.

Alltop.com takes a step up from a simple search engine to curate the day's hottest headlines in a given category. They pull their articles from the best-rated sites and most followed blogs in the industry. It's a simple approach that says, "You don't have time to wade through mountains of data to find the gold nuggets. Let us do it for you." Unless you're bored and want to read the bad and the boring along with the good and the great, stop by Alltop today.

There are plenty of other sites offering similar services, but if you're looking for inspiration, number 5 on our list is simple networking. Join group boards on Pinterest, gather up your groupies in Facebook land, or just meet some friends at a local café and brainstorm. Sometimes, it's not about finding the new content; it's about having the great idea that creates it! You're amazing! You got that, right?

ABOUT THE AUTHOR

Tamparey Jones-Davis is a creative writing author, Life and Business coach, and successful online Boutique Owner.

She is the founder of Biz OwnHers and specializes in Goal setting and coaching others to gain clarity and focus on their life goals. She is a firm believer of the law of attraction and manifestation which she uses to lead her readers in her first book Goal Digging. She is currently working on her forth book and building her blog Biz OwnHers. Her mission is to empower people to take control of their financial future, experience the entrepreneur lifestyle, and live life to the fullest.

www.ingramcontent.com/pod-product-compliance
Lightning Source LLC
Chambersburg PA
CBHW071304220526
45468CB00001B/261